JUDGES

THE GUIDE

JUDGES

Peter Bloomfield

EP — EVANGELICAL PRESS

EP EVANGELICAL PRESS

Evangelical Press
Faverdale North, Darlington, DL3 0PH England
Evangelical Press USA
PO Box 825, Webster NY 14580 USA
email: sales@evangelical-press.org
www.evangelicalpress.org

'The Guide' web site: **www.evangelicalpress.org/TheGuide**

Published by Evangelical Press
First published 2005

© Evangelical Press 2005. All rights reserved. No part of this publication may be reproduced, stored in a retrieval system or transmitted, in any form, or by any means, electronic, mechanical, photocopying, recording or otherwise, without the prior permission of the publishers.

All scripture quotations, unless otherwise indicated, are taken from the Holy Bible, New International Version. Copyright 1973, 1978, 1984, International Bible Society. Used by permission of the Hodder Headline Group. All rights reserved.

British Library Cataloguing in Publication Data available
ISBN 0 85234 571 2

CONTENTS

How to use *The Guide*   8

1. **Understanding Judges (An overview)**   11
   The author
   The layout
   The lessons

2. **The rot sets in!** (1:1–3:6)   25
   Background promises
   Broken promises
   Bokim promises

3. **The angel of the LORD** (2, 6, 13)   41
   He is God
   He is God-sent

4. **Christ: The angel of the LORD** (Exod. 3:1–15)   55
   Identity of functions
   Identity of names
   Identity of testaments

5. **An old soldier and an oxgoad** (3:7–11,31)   67
   Othniel the old soldier
   Shamgar and the oxgoad

6. **A pointed message from God** (3:12–30)   79
   The events
   The ethics
   The edification

7. **Barak and Deborah in concert** (4–5)   95
   The end of peace
   The end of oppression
   The end of Sisera

8. **Learning from Gideon (Part 1)** (6:1–7:15)   111
   Spiritual preparation
   Military preparation
   Emotional preparation

9. **Learning from Gideon (Part 2)** (7:16–8:35)   125
   His victory
   His wisdom
   His folly

10. **A thorny problem** (9)   139
    Get the picture
    Get the point

11. **Has Jephthah been defamed?** (10–12)   151
    Consider the scene
    Consider his character
    Consider his vow

12. **What about Samson? (Part 1)** (13–16)   167
    Is Samson in heaven?
    Is Samson naturally strong?
    Is Samson a type of Christ?

13. **What about Samson? (Part 2)** (13–16)   183
    A lone-ranger man
    A faithful man
    A misunderstood man

14. **Final flashbacks** (17–18)   197
    Private corruption (family level)
    Official corruption (religious level)
    Tribal corruption (social level)

15. **No king — do anything!** (19)   209
    'Baptized sodomy'
    Wilful sodomy
    Cursed sodomy

16. **A stitch in time** (20)   223
    It was true for them
    It is true for us

17. **Legalism to the rescue!** (21)   235
    Legalism in Israel
    Legalism in the church
    In closing

Appendix — The monarchy: an issue resolved   247

Notes   251

HOW TO USE *THE GUIDE*

Judges is the latest in a series of books called *The Guide*. This series covers books of the Bible on an individual basis, such as Ecclesiastes and Job, and relevant topics, such as creation, stewardship and Christian comfort. The objective of the series is to communicate the Christian faith in a straightforward and readable way and encourage believers to live out their faith.

To help you to study the Word of God more deeply, each book in *The Guide* series has relatively short and concise chapters with questions at the end of each chapter for personal study or group discussion.

An innovative and exciting feature of *The Guide* is that it is linked to its own web site. As well as being encouraged to search God's Word for yourself, you are invited to ask questions related to the book on the web site, where you will not only have your own questions answered, but you can also see a selection of answers that have been given to other readers. The web site can be found at *www.evangelicalpress.org/TheGuide*. Once you are on the site you just need to click on the 'select' button at the top of the page and choose the book on which you wish to post a question. Your question will then be answered either by Michael Bentley, the web site coordinator and author of *Colossians and Philemon*, or others who have been selected because of their experience and understanding of the Word of God and their dedication to working for the glory of the Lord.

There are other titles in line to be published in *The Guide* series and with the positive feedback and popularity of our interactive web site, we hope to continue that into the future.

It is the publisher's hope that you will be stirred to think more deeply about the Christian faith and that you will be helped and encouraged — through the study of God's Word — in living your Christian life. We live in demanding days and we need the firm compass of the Word of God to give us direction and practical encouragement as we navigate the complexities of this new millennium and pursue the glory of our God.

www.evangelicalpress.org/TheGuide

THE GUIDE

CHAPTER ONE

UNDERSTANDING JUDGES (AN OVERVIEW)

THE GUIDE

LOOK IT UP

BIBLE READING

Judges 2:6–23

INTRODUCTION

Most Christians know very little about the book of Judges. What is its point and purpose and its role among the sixty-six inspired books? What is God saying in this portion of his Word? The more *exciting* stories of Gideon and Samson typify the few things that people might remember, but the book as a whole is unfamiliar. Why is this so? Several factors explain why this book has been sadly neglected.

To begin with it is neither a pleasant nor an enjoyable read. It is a hard book about hard times, showing sin in all its repulsiveness. Even more uncomfortable for us, it mainly deals with wickedness among the people of God. Because there is essentially one church throughout all ages, the mess confronted by the judges in Israel is the mess in our own family tree. The book makes no attempt to be cosmetic. It openly portrays ungodliness among the people of God. The modern church cannot read the book of Judges without being implicated. We too are unfaithful to Jehovah. We too are unholy. We too are disobedient and compromised and can grieve the

Holy Spirit. Therefore, reading this book pricks our conscience. Perhaps that is why it is neglected. You do not hear many sermons or read many books about the book of Judges because it comes painfully close to the bone.

> **THINK ABOUT IT**
>
> The most unpleasant truths can be the most needed and, therefore, cannot afford to be neglected. They do not go away by ignoring them. As God's Word it is profitable for teaching, correction and training in righteousness. When the lessons of history in the Old Testament are neglected its mistakes will inevitably be repeated. It is an old book, thirty centuries removed from us, but it speaks powerfully to our generation. While it reveals the marvellous grace of God it also warns against presumption. It is exactly the message needed by the modern church. Indeed, if the church today hearkened to this book it would not be as worldly and compromised as it often appears to be.

Paradoxically God's people are often weakest at moments of greatest privilege and blessing. There is a marked contrast between God's people during the time of Judges and those led by Joshua just a generation earlier. In Joshua's time the people had obeyed God and entered and possessed the promised land. One enemy after another fell before the army of God. It was a time of unprecedented conquest and privilege. They were not perfect, but everything pointed to a new era of godliness in Canaan. The new foundations being laid would surely be those of the city of God. But this was not the case. As soon as Joshua and his generation died, Israel became wicked: 'After that whole generation had been gathered to their fathers, another generation grew up, who knew neither the LORD nor what he had done for Israel. Then the Israelites did evil in the eyes of the LORD and served the Baals' (2:10–11). The book of Judges spans a long period of about 350 years — from Joshua to Samuel — or a quarter of Old Testament history. We can only neglect so much divine revelation at our loss.

The author

The author of the book of Judges is anonymous, but the Jewish tradition claiming Samuel as the author seems very likely. It had to be written by someone looking back over the whole pre-kingdom period because of the repeated statement, 'Israel had no king' (17:6; 18:1; 19:1; 21:25). Israel had its first king (Saul) in 1050 B.C. Jerusalem still belonged to the Jebusites at the time the book of Judges was written (1:21). This dates it prior to 1004 B.C., when David made Jerusalem the Jewish capital (2 Sam. 5:5–9).[1]

Considering these facts the book of Judges must have been written early in Jewish history, approximately 1000 B.C., about the time of Saul or David's early years, in the days of Samuel.[2]

The layout

To gain an appreciation of the book of Judges, it is helpful to understand both its layout and its lessons. This book has a definite structure. It falls into three distinct sections.

The introduction

This introductory section (1:1–3:6) serves two purposes. First, it links up with Joshua by continuing from where that book ended. It shows that God was still fighting for Israel and driving out their enemies before them. The Israelites were continuing to occupy and subdue the promised land. Joshua was gone, but God was not, neither was his blessing, nor his covenant nor the duties facing Israel.

Second, the introduction sets the scene for everything in the book by explaining Israel's short-lived obedience after Joshua died. Even the generation that buried Joshua was only partially obedient to God. The first chapter records the failures of one tribe after another, starting with the failure of Judah, then Benjamin, Joseph, Zebulun, Asher, Naphtali and Dan. That is why the angel of the LORD rebuked them at Bokim. But the next generation was much worse:

WHAT THE TEXT TEACHES

Joshua ... the servant of the LORD, died at the age of a hundred and ten ... After that whole generation had been gathered to their fathers, another generation grew up, who knew neither the LORD nor what he had done for Israel. Then the Israelites did evil in the eyes of the LORD and served the Baals (2:8–11).

Reading further reveals the sad picture of Israel's rapid decline after Joshua: 'They forsook the LORD, the God of their fathers, who had brought them out of Egypt. They followed and worshipped various gods of the peoples around them' (2:12). They participated in the religion of the Canaanite male and female idols: 'They provoked the LORD to anger because they forsook him and served Baal and the Ashtoreths' (2:12–13).

REMEMBER THIS

The introduction provides us with a vital key to the book by outlining something we see over and over again in a cycle of four steps:

1. The Israelites sin, forsaking the ways of the Lord (2:11–13)
2. Enemies oppress them (2:14–15)
3. They cry out in distress to the Lord (2:15,18)
4. The Lord saves them, raising up a deliverer (a judge) (2:16)

This cycle happened repeatedly. As soon as the judge who delivered them had died, God's people acted corruptly again — even more corruptly: 'But when the judge died, the people returned to ways even more corrupt than those of their fathers, following other gods and serving and worshipping them. They refused to give up their evil practices and stubborn ways' (2:19). Therefore God left certain enemy nations in the promised land to test Israel: the Philistines, Canaanites, Sidonians, Hivites, Hittites, Amorites, Perizzites and Jebusites are named. It is a sobering principle: if the people of God are not strongly committed to God, he may strengthen their enemies. Wickedness has serious consequences. God can put weapons in the hands of our enemies. They will advance, and the people of God will go backwards.

The repeated cycles

Judges 3:7 to the end of chapter 16 details the repeated cycles of sin, chastisement, pity and deliverance. The first cycle is described in chapter 3:

> The Israelites did evil in the eyes of the LORD; they forgot the LORD their God and served the Baals and the Asherahs. The anger of the LORD burned against Israel so that he sold them into the hands of Cushan-Rishathaim king of Aram Naharaim, to whom the Israelites were subject for eight years. But when they cried out to the LORD, he raised up for them a deliverer, Othniel son of Kenaz, Caleb's

younger brother, who saved them. The Spirit of the LORD came upon him, so that he became Israel's judge and went to war. The LORD gave Cushan-Rishathaim king of Aram into the hands of Othniel, who overpowered him. So the land had peace for forty years, until Othniel son of Kenaz died (3:7–11).

The Othniel cycle is the first one in the pattern. Later we will study selections from the rest of this large section. The other leaders are Ehud, Shamgar, Deborah, Gideon, Jephthah and Samson. Altogether thirteen judges are mentioned, but only the victories of these seven are described in any detail.[3]

The Hebrew title for the book is 'Judges' (שֹׁפְטִים), but we need to avoid reading our modern meaning (magistrates) into it.[4] In the book of Judges the primary emphasis is not on *magistrate* but *saviour*. The judges of Israel were the heroes who liberated God's people from oppression. Although they ruled and led in a general sense, the judges were primarily saviours. They typify Christ, the ultimate Saviour of God's people. God mercifully raised up judge-deliverers in times of crisis. God's Holy Spirit came mightily on them, equipping them for tremendous acts of political and military victory over their enemies. This book repeatedly proves the faithfulness of our covenant-keeping God. He said, 'I will never break my covenant with you but you have not obeyed me' (2:1–2). In the face of such perverse people we might expect God to dismiss them once and for all, but he is faithful to his promise. He preserves a remnant, the covenant family from whom Christ (the Messiah) will finally come.

The appendix

The appendix (chapters 17 to 21) describes two very sinful episodes in Israel at that time.

In chapters 17 and 18 a man called Micah not only stole money from his mother but also made a graven image to worship. He started his own cult and hired his own personal Levite (priest) to officiate. The tribe of Dan spread this idolatry further.

Chapters 19 to 21 tell a most gruesome story of a Levite who carved up the body of his concubine into twelve pieces, sending the grisly parcels throughout the whole land, one piece to each tribe. The result was civil war, eleven tribes of Israel against one tribe, Benjamin. We will consider these things in due course, but, for now, two comments are in order.

First, the book does not read in chronological order as if the events in the appendix happened after Samson. The evidence suggests that the incidents happened very early in the history of the judges. They were put at the end of the book so as not to interfere with the record of the various cycles of Judges.

Second, these events are recorded to show us the extent of depravity in Israel. The appendix mentions examples of theft, idolatry, immorality, homosexuality, abduction and butchery. The book concludes with a disgraceful example of legalism, a problem that occurs frequently throughout church history. Thirty centuries later we are still very good at using the law to evade the law. Angry vows taken at Mizpah during the civil war soon got Israel into a bind. Rather than admitting error and repenting, legalism came to the rescue. Their pedantic ingenuity of straining at gnats and swallowing camels would dwarf many Pharisees. It is a sick people that resort to semantic definitions of its own rules to avoid admitting guilt, but it happens. We will consider more examples in due course.

The lessons

The book of Judges illustrates that God's people need a leader. Sheep are lost without a shepherd. The 350 years of anarchy were preparation for a monarchy. Joshua provided good leadership, but when he died the tribes became disunited and individuals began to live as they pleased. The leadership of the judges over the next three to four centuries gave some relief, but it was temporary and partial. As soon as the judges died the old weaknesses set in again.

The judges were preparing Israel for the next period in salvation history — the kingdom period. However, even the best of the kings needed a greater king and head. They all failed at some point. They did not provide an exemplary reign over God's people. The whole Old Testament is preparing us for that righteous, messianic king, Jesus Christ. He is the King of kings, the great Judge-Deliverer and the ultimate Saviour. He alone is the head (Lord) of the church. When we disobey him and do what is right in our own eyes we repeat the history of the book of Judges. To the extent that we submit to Christ as King we will be blessed of God. To the extent that we refuse obedience, we can expect our enemies to overpower us. Three lessons are especially appropriate.

Let us note that a glorious history is no safeguard for a church. Sin still crouches at the door seeking to devour us. Despite all of its glorious history, Israel sinned. Despite a great leader like Joshua and miraculous deliverances, they repeatedly forgot the Lord. Reviving our historical roots does not guarantee God's good pleasure. We may be able to trace our roots back to Reformation giants like Wycliffe, Huss, Calvin, Knox and Chalmers. Perhaps we can point to numerous blessings from the hand of God. But Israel had a fabulous history too. It had Abraham, Moses, Joshua and Samuel, but look how low it sank! Reformation in the past does not prevent deformation in the present.

REMEMBER THIS

We must examine ourselves as we are now, not as we once were in history. Are we now walking according to the law of

REMEMBER THIS

the Lord? Let us never glory in past heroes. This book does not glory in the judges. It shows them 'warts and all'. It is not uncommon for readers to be perplexed at the candid way various weaknesses of the judges are narrated, including Gideon's fleece and Samson's moral lapses. The greatest heroes in Israel had serious weaknesses, yet God condescended to use them. Noah got drunk and David committed adultery and murder. There is only one in whom we may boast and glory — Jesus Christ our Lord. Only in him is there no spot or blemish, no weakness and no failure or disappointment. Let us be done with an unhealthy glorying in mere men. We thank God for the gifts that he gave them and for the contributions that they have made, but let Christians glory in Christ — never in Calvin or Moses or Joshua or Samson.

We should also learn that it is critical for the church to train its children well. This book tells us that problems developed because 'another generation grew up, who knew neither the LORD nor what he had done for Israel' (2:10). It seems that parents did not nurture their children diligently in the things of God, and so they grew into an ignorant, godless, iniquitous generation. Yes, they had some basic head knowledge of their religion. They knew to cry out to Jehovah when the pressure was on, but they had not been well established in faithfulness. Their religion was superficial. Their parents had not provided consistent role models (as the first chapter demonstrates). Psalm 78 reflects on this lamentable failure of parents not training up children in the ways of God. It is not enough just to teach them the true ways of God in the Bible. We must live it out before them and with them, as consistent mentors, or of course they will go astray. They will provoke God to wrath, and their blood will be on our hands — at least to the extent that we set them a poor example.

Above all, the lesson of this book is that the people of God survive only because of his amazing grace. None of us can stand in our own strength or on our own merits. This book repeatedly highlights God's incredible patience and pity. Time after time God raised up judges to deliver rebellious people. It was sheer grace. It was never because they behaved any better and never because they turned away from their sins. The only change in them was their moaning as they cried to the Lord: 'For the LORD had compassion on them as they groaned under those who oppressed and afflicted them' (2:18). Our God is abundant in mercy, and when he gives it, it is never deserved. This is the gospel of grace, which is so clearly displayed in this book.

Therefore, if you feel undeserving of God's mercy, do not let that stop you from seeking it. We still live in the days of grace. God can still be moved to pity as he proved at Calvary. He is abundant in mercy, but be careful. His Spirit will not strive with men forever. The doors of mercy will one day be shut firm. Anyone who is locked out of heaven has certainly provoked God to wrath, over and over again. Those who weary even the patience of God are wretched indeed! The God revealed in the book of Judges is lovely. May this overview help us to see him more clearly.

QUESTIONS FOR DISCUSSION

1. In the light of the facts recorded in Isaiah 53:3,5 and Matthew 27:20–50, what do you think about the statement: The gospel itself is not always pleasant reading?

2. How are the main features of a proper view of ancient history identified in 1 Corinthians 10:1–2 and Hebrews 3:7–4:11?

3. Godly pedagogy is mentoring more than teaching. What light does Deuteronomy 6 shed on this opinion?

THE GUIDE

CHAPTER TWO

THE ROT SETS IN!

BIBLE READING

Judges 1:1–3:6

The writer of Judges begins by describing the rapid decline of the people of God. Although the collapse of Jericho's walls was less than a generation earlier, those heady days of conquest seemed far away. These early days of the judges are when *the rot sets in*! As always, unfaithfulness eats the heart out of a church. In this case it was unfaithfulness to certain promises. A proper understanding of Judges requires a knowledge of background promises, broken promises and Bokim promises.

Background promises

The background involves God's covenant promises. Apart from them it is impossible to understand the issues here. God had commanded the Hebrew people to destroy all the former inhabitants of the promised land. They were not to spare them or make pacts or treaties with them. God was quite emphatic about this:

However, in the cities of the nations the LORD your God is giving you as an inheritance, do not leave alive anything that breathes. Completely destroy them — the Hittites, Amorites, Canaanites, Perizzites, Hivites and Jebusites — as the LORD your God has commanded you. Otherwise, they will teach you to follow all the detestable things they do in worshipping their gods, and you will sin against the LORD your God (Deut. 20:16–18).

There was nothing ambiguous about it:

Destroy completely all the places on the high mountains and on the hills and under every spreading tree where the nations you are dispossessing worship their gods. Break down their altars, smash their sacred stones and burn their Asherah poles in the fire; cut down the idols of their gods and wipe out their names from those places' (Deut. 12:2–3; see also Num. 33:51–55).

Joshua was there on the day that God said these things, and when they went into the promised land he was scrupulously faithful to obey: 'So Joshua subdued the whole region, including the hill country, the Negev, the western foothills and the mountain slopes, together with all their kings. He left no survivors. He totally destroyed all who breathed, just as the LORD, the God of Israel, had commanded' (Josh. 10:40).

There is nothing unfair or harsh in this; however, some people point to these parts of the Old Testament and condemn what Joshua did. They denounce the Jewish conquest of Canaan as inherently wrong. They criticize the Bible as being the cause of wars and hostility. They invoke a sort of 'native title' principle, as if antiquity grants perpetual ownership. They forget that: 'The earth is the LORD's, and everything in it, the world, and all who live in it; for he founded it upon the seas and established it upon the waters' (Ps. 24:1–2). Because God owns Canaan, he exercised his sovereign rights when he gave it to his people. He insisted on no compromise with the godless.

We must remember that Joshua and his men were acting as God's agents and not conducting private business. They were not settling personal scores against Canaan but were the instruments of divine justice. This important context is revealed in the background promises in Genesis 15, the promises God gave to Abraham, namely:

> Know for certain that your descendants will be strangers in a country not their own, and they will be enslaved and mistreated four hundred years. But I will punish the nation they serve as slaves, and afterward they will come out with great possessions… In the fourth generation your descendants will come back here, for the sin of the

Amorites has not yet reached its full measure (Gen. 15:13–16).

It is clear that 'the Amorites' represent the inhabitants of the whole land of Canaan (see Gen. 15:18–21).

Notice God's patience. Although the Canaanites were incredibly wicked God said that he would give them another 400 years before judging them, even though he knew that they would only get worse during that time. Anyone who knows the disgraceful habits of the Canaanite peoples during those four centuries would agree that they were ripe for judgement. The sin of the Amorites had certainly reached full measure by the time of Joshua.

God deliberately underscored this fact when the Law was given, even threatening to take the land from Israel if they disobeyed him. His language is vivid:

> Do not defile yourselves in any of these ways, because this is how the nations that I am going to drive out before you became defiled. Even the land was defiled; so I punished it for its sin, and the land vomited out its inhabitants. But you must keep my decrees and my laws. The native-born and the aliens living among you must not do any of these detestable things, for all these things were done by the people who lived in the land before you, and the land became defiled. And if you defile the land, it will vomit you out as it vomited out the nations that were before you. Everyone

WHAT THE TEXT TEACHES

who does any of these detestable things — such persons must be cut off from their people. Keep my requirements and do not follow any of the detestable customs that were practiced before you came and do not defile yourselves with them. I am the LORD your God (Lev. 18:24–30).

The Bible describes the detestable religious practices and vulgar lifestyle of these nations. Leviticus 18 lists their gruesome sins, including homosexuality and bestiality. One of the most repulsive things was the worship of Molech, a carved statue with a hollow stomach cavity where fires were lit. Little children were burned alive in the flames of his belly. Far from being harsh, if Joshua and the Hebrews had spared these nations they would have demonstrated a light-hearted view of sin. They would have trifled with the justice of God. Because these nations were so revolting God describes the land as spewing them up, like a stomach vomiting up its nauseating contents.

REMEMBER THIS

There can be no valid complaint against the conquest of Canaan because it was God's holy judgement. Joshua's armies were simply God's instruments. The Bible repeatedly stresses this fact.

> God told Israel, 'I brought you to the land of the Amorites who lived east of the Jordan. They fought against you, but I gave them into your hands. I destroyed them from before you, and you took possession of their land' (Josh. 24:8). Joshua also reminded them of that fact: 'You yourselves have seen everything the LORD your God has done to all these nations for your sake; it was the LORD your God who fought for you' (Josh. 23:3). It is a sobering fact that unless we interpret history consistent with Bible teaching we are in danger of condemning God.

Let us not forget these background truths. The almighty God is free to send whatever instruments he chooses to punish wicked nations — plagues, floods, droughts, earthquakes or armies. Joshua was the captain of such an army. The Jewish conquest of Canaan fulfilled the background promises given to Abraham.

Broken promises

Not content to forget God's promises, the people also made their own promises and promptly broke them. We see it in Joshua's farewell address. He declared his allegiance to God: 'But as for me and my house, we will serve the LORD' (Josh. 24:15). This prompted the people of Israel to make a similar promise:

> Far be it from us to forsake the LORD to serve other gods! It was the LORD our God himself who brought

us and our fathers up out of Egypt, from that land of slavery, and performed those great signs before our eyes. He protected us on our entire journey and among all the nations through which we travelled. And the LORD drove out before us all the nations, including the Amorites, who lived in the land. We too will serve the LORD, because he is our God (Josh. 24:16–18).

Joshua's reply was candid. Rather than the expected congratulations, Joshua confronted them: 'You are not able to serve the LORD. He is a holy God; he is a jealous God. He will not forgive your rebellion and your sins' (Josh. 24:19). He sensed that the people were too sure of themselves. Joshua warned them that serving Jehovah is not an easy thing. He is holy and he demands wholehearted service. He is jealous, demanding a denial of all false religions. He expects his servants to turn away from sin. In making this promise, Israel overlooked its tendency to sin. They were too confident, and their promise just rolled glibly off their tongue: 'Far be it from us to forsake the LORD to serve other gods!' (Josh. 24:16). No, not us! It was similar for Peter much later in history. He promised never to forsake Jesus even if all other men did. He had to be similarly warned by One greater than Joshua. Jesus told Peter that he would not be able to keep his promise: 'Before the rooster crows, you will disown me three times' (Matt. 26:34).

Israel simply dismissed Joshua's words and said, 'No! We will serve the LORD' (Josh. 24:21). So Joshua spelled out the solemnity of their promise by two actions. First he put it into hard copy, permanently recorded in the book of the law: 'On that day Joshua made a covenant for the people, and there at Shechem he drew up for them decrees and laws. And Joshua recorded these things in the Book of the Law of God' (Josh. 24:25–26).

Second, a large stone monument was set up next to the place of worship:

> Then he took a large stone and set it up there under the oak near the holy place of the LORD. 'See!' he said to all the people. 'This stone will be a witness against us. It has heard all the words the LORD has said to us. It will be a witness against you if you are untrue to your God' (Josh. 24:26–27).

We could be forgiven for hoping that this was the beginning of a very bright chapter in the history of redemption. It seemed that the people of God were on the threshold of victory. Even greater things were expected. But alas, it was not so! The book of Joshua ends there and Judges immediately shows us how these promises were broken — not sporadically or rarely but repeatedly, brazenly and grievously broken. Why? The two main causes were partial obedience and worldly compromise.

How common it is to selectively obey God when it suits us. The opening words of the book of Judges illustrate this (1:4–7). Israel won the battle at Bezek, but instead of killing the pagan king, Adoni-Bezek, as God commanded, they cut off his thumbs and big toes and spared him. Perhaps Israel had logical and plausible reasons for doing this. He would know the land and the strengths and weaknesses of other kings and nations. Maybe he would be a good source of military intelligence to help in future battles. Or perhaps they thought that death was too good for this man. They would treat him with his own medicine, mutilating him exactly the same way that he admitted to the mutilation of seventy other kings (1:7).

<u>Whatever their reason, unfaithfulness is sin. We can never be wiser than God and never more just.</u> By cutting off his thumbs and big toes Israel was adopting a Canaanite practice that was common in the pagan world. It ended a man's military career. He could never again pick up a sword or swing it without thumbs. He could neither hold a bow and arrow nor draw the string effectively. Without big toes he could not run to fight in a battle. Clearly then, Israel broke its promises and behaved like pagans.

In a second example of <u>partial obedience</u> Israel captured the hill country of Gaza, Ashkelon and Ekron, but failed to drive out the inhabitants of the valley because they had iron chariots (1:19). Chariots had not been a problem to Joshua. He had defeated a massive confederate army with many horses and chariots: 'as numerous as the sand on the seashore' (Josh. 11:4). Also,

Deborah was soon to lead Israel victoriously against Sisera's 900 iron chariots (Judg. 4). However, God has a promise for exactly this situation: 'When you go to war against your enemies and see horses and chariots and an army greater than yours, do not be afraid of them, because the LORD your God, who brought you up out of Egypt, will be with you' (Deut. 20:1).

Worldly compromise was the other means of breaking promises. Israel compromised with the world making agreements with the people of the land. They negotiated forms of peaceful coexistence. The writer shows how tribe after tribe compromised (1:16–36). For instance: 'The Benjamites, however, failed to dislodge the Jebusites, who were living in Jerusalem; to this day the Jebusites live there with the Benjamites' (1:21). In other words they were content for the enemies of God to remain comfortable in the land.

Such compromise allowed their enemies to revive. For instance, the Amorites persisted in living in Mt Heres, Aijalon and Shaalbim (1:35). What was Aijalon? It was the place of one of Israel's great victories a few years earlier, the place where Joshua commanded the sun and moon to stand still. Thus the place where Canaan was recently humiliated in defeat was now the venue for regaining a foothold.

To summarize

Israel was setting itself up for soft living. God's people refused to battle against iron chariots, keeping their enemies alive as home helpers and slaves. They looked for easier ways of serving God than he had commanded. Like most sin in the church, it starts in small matters and gets worse over time. So it was in Israel. The writer shows that their promised loyalty was gone. The previous generation had promised: 'Far be it from us to forsake the LORD to serve other gods!' (Josh. 24:16) and 'We will serve the LORD our God and obey him' (Josh. 24:24). But now '…they forsook him and served Baal and the Ashtoreths.'

THINK ABOUT IT

The church on paper is not the same as the church in action. The confessional standards (what we say we believe) can be very good, as was the case in Joshua 24. But a good confession and great historical documents do not guarantee that a church is sound. Plenty of churches give lip service to the excellent *Westminster Confession*. They promise it, but they break it. Married couples make very good promises at their wedding. They make vows pledging to be faithful to their spouse as long as they live, but broken marriages testify to numerous broken violations. This is when the rot sets in — when promises are neglected.

Bokim promises

Bokim is the Jewish word for weepers. The angel of the LORD appeared there and gave them promises of trouble and affliction, *Bokim promises*. God promised that the Canaanites, who they had sinfully tolerated, would now become thorns in Israel's side, and their idols and religions would become snares and traps (2:3). All sin has its consequences, and even when God mercifully forgives, sin leaves its scars and consequences in this life.

We read that the angel of the LORD came up from Gilgal to Bokim. I mention this because it points out the decline in Israel's condition. When this angel last appeared to them it was at Gilgal, as Captain of the Hosts (Josh. 5). Gilgal was the first place in Canaan where the Hebrews rested after crossing the Jordan. There they entered into God's promised rest. There they had their first meal of rich foods in the land flowing with milk and honey. There the manna stopped — the bread from heaven that fed them during forty years of wilderness wanderings. There the angel of the LORD assured them that he was for them: he was on their side.

But now the angel comes to Bokim against them, and his promised affliction was a reality as these words so grimly testify: 'Whenever Israel went out to fight, the hand of the LORD was against them to defeat them, just as he had sworn to them. They were in great distress' (2:15).

Bokim is where the holy and jealous God promised to withdraw his blessings, grace, favour and power from the disobedient Israel. The Bokim promises are not just for the age of the judges. They solemnly warn every age of humanity not to carry the name of the Lord God in vain. In Ephesians 4 we are warned not to grieve this jealous God, this Holy Spirit. A grieved Spirit is often a withdrawn Spirit.

Jesus gives us the latest version of the Bokim promises: 'Repent ... If you do not repent, I will come to you and remove your lampstand from its place' (Rev. 2:5). 'Repent therefore! Otherwise, I will soon come to you and will fight against them with the sword of my mouth' (Rev. 2:16). 'But if you do not wake up, I will come like a thief, and you will not know at what time I will come to you' (Rev. 3:3).

Bokim is, in effect, God warning his people: You think that you know better than I do. You would not remove the enemy. This will cost you dearly. These areas of unfaithfulness in your life are going to drag you down, being a constant nuisance and snare to you.

If we will not act in obedience to the whole counsel of God let no one be surprised if the church is 'sold ... to their enemies all around, whom they were no longer able to resist' (2:14). Of course our task is not identical to Joshua's. The New Testament church has no mandate to fight and conquer nations. But the essential principles of the gospel are the same. Are we afraid to take on certain 'iron chariots'? Do we leave apostate thinking untouched and unchallenged, whether it is in the field of medicine, geology or history? Are we ashamed of the gospel? A pietistic church concerned only with souls being saved has abandoned a large part of its mandate. If the church is not obedient to every instruction of the King in every corner of the land what does it matter if it has a good creed?

May we honestly examine ourselves to see if we have departed in any way from obeying God. If we have, then that is where the rot sets in! Even if it is only one small spot, it will spread. The book of Judges shows two great options for the people of God in every age. There is a potential for either greatness (if we are faithful) or catastrophe (if we ignore the lessons in Judges).

QUESTIONS FOR DISCUSSION

1. *God had various motives in his determination to destroy Canaanite culture. Which motives are implied in the following texts: Psalm 115:1–10; Ezekiel 18:23–25; Genesis 15:13–16; Deuteronomy 12:2–3 and 20:16–18?*

2. *In what forms does the sin of selective obedience occur in the following texts: Malachi 1; Isaiah 1:10–17 and Revelation 2:12–29?*

3. *Growth in godliness of character is essentially a lifelong pursuit. How is this reinforced in Philippians 3:10–19; 2 Peter 1:1–11 and Hebrews 12:14?*

THE GUIDE

CHAPTER THREE

THE ANGEL OF THE LORD

BIBLE READING

Judges 2, 6 and 13

We must now deal with the intriguing personage called *malach Yahweh*, 'the angel of the LORD'. We meet him at key points in the Old Testament. Great awe and mystery surround him. Who is he, and how are we to understand him? We meet him first in Genesis 16 talking to Hagar. He is the same one with whom Jacob wrestled (Gen. 32). He is also the one who appeared to Moses in the burning bush (Exod. 3:2). He is the one who spoke to Abraham when he was offering up Isaac on Mt Moriah (Gen. 22). He appears again in Joshua 5:14 as the 'commander of the army of the LORD'.

He features large in the book of Judges. In Judges 2:1 we read, 'the angel of the LORD went up from Gilgal to Bokim'. There he chastised Israel for their sin. We meet him again in chapter 6 with Gideon and in chapter 13 with Manoah and his wife (Samson's parents). He acts with divine authority at every point. The last book of the Old Testament refers to him as 'the messenger [angel] of the covenant' (Mal. 3:1; see chapter 4 for further details).

The weight of evidence forces us to conclude that the angel of the LORD is Jehovah himself. More specifically he is the pre-incarnate Messiah, the second person of the Godhead, temporarily appearing in human form. It is Christ leading his Old Testament church before his incarnation in the womb of the virgin Mary. We will consider the evidence in the next chapter. The present task is to demonstrate proof for the assertion that the angel of the LORD *is* the LORD.

THINK ABOUT IT

Malach Yahweh is *Yahweh*. He *is* the almighty God. He *is* divine. He does not merely represent the Lord — he *is* the Lord. He does not merely speak for Jehovah — he *is* Jehovah speaking. He is not merely a created angel but the creator of angels. Admittedly this raises a question: *If the angel is God then why is he called an angel?* The answer follows after the proof of his deity.

Before proceeding, it is important to consider earlier revelations of the angel of the LORD in texts prior to those in the book of Judges. Those chronologically earlier texts include Genesis 16, 22 and 32 and Exodus 3. We need to start there because the progress of that revelation is implied in Judges. The interpretation of the angel of the LORD in the Judges texts depends on those earlier texts. As we will see, a good example occurs in the case of Gideon. This systematic and orderly approach has gospel significance. It provides a credible exegetical basis for interpreting the angel of the LORD as a theophany (an appearance of God) or, more precisely, a Christophany (an appearance of Christ).

A helpful way of starting is to recognize a key fact about this Hebrew word *malach* (מַלְאָךְ), angel. It is used 214 times in the Old Testament. In fifty per cent of these cases it refers to ordinary men, like you and me, who acted as messengers for other people. For example: 'Jacob sent messengers ahead of him to his brother Esau' (Gen. 32:3). Only seventeen per cent of the time does it refer to what we commonly call 'angels' (heaven's angels like Gabriel). In the other thirty-three per cent of cases it refers to this special character that we are interested in now, the angel of the LORD.

Our culture predisposes us to a biased idea of an angel (*malach*). The word itself triggers our thoughts towards those non-human, spiritual beings around the throne of God. But *malach* is a very general and common Hebrew word for messenger. In about 100 places the Old Testament calls ordinary people like us (even slaves and servants) 'angels'. God's prophets are called 'angels' in several places. For example: 'Then Haggai, the LORD's messenger (angel of the LORD), gave this message' (Hag. 1:13). Haggai is literally called '*malach Yahweh*'.

The point is that the word *malach* (angel) essentially refers to the task of a servant delivering a message. In itself the word does not tell us about the nature of the person performing the task. That depends entirely on the context. Jacob's errand boys were 'angels' but not in the sense that Gabriel is. Gabriel is an angel but in a different sense than Haggai. And we shall see that the angel of the LORD is God's messenger in a different sense to any other. We must not think only of spiritual creatures like seraphim when we read the word 'angel'. Our problem is that because we are reading Hebrew literature translated into English, we tend to transport our English concepts into Hebrew thought. But our word 'angel' is far more specific than the Hebrew word it translates. There are two key facts to grasp about this character called *malach Yahweh*. He is God, and he is God-sent.

He is God

The Bible's first reference to God as 'the angel of the LORD' is in the story of Hagar (Gen. 16). He appeared to an unhappy Hagar giving her instructions and encouragement. 'The angel of the LORD found Hagar near a spring in the desert' (Gen. 16:7). There was a conversation between them. The writer (Moses) gave his inspired comment in verse 13: 'She gave this name to the LORD who spoke to her: "You are the God who sees me"' (אֵל רֳאִי). This could be translated as 'You are the seeing God' or 'You, God, see!'

The point is that Hagar knows that she has been talking with God. She knows that the angel of the LORD *is* the

WHAT THE TEXT TEACHES

LORD, so she gives him God's name. She was amazed to remain alive after seeing him: 'Have I even remained alive here after seeing Him?' (Gen. 16:13, NASB). This fear of death is common to those who have seen God in some way. Jacob, Manoah's wife, Isaiah and John were all afraid when they saw God.

Some try to avoid this conclusion by saying that an emotional Hagar made an honest mistake in thinking that she saw and heard Jehovah. But this is untenable because Moses himself drew the same conclusion. It was Moses, after the event and in a sober and deliberate testimony, who asserts that it was Jehovah who spoke to Hagar. Moses, writing under the guidance of the Holy Spirit, tells us, 'She gave this name to the LORD who spoke to her: "You are the God who sees me"' (Gen. 16:13). This has major implications for the Christian faith.

THINK ABOUT IT

The integrity of Scripture is at stake here! You cannot have only a mistaken Hagar: you have to live with a mistaken Moses too! You have to say that the Bible is wrong, which means that you reject the Christian faith. So Genesis 16 is 'Exhibit A', where Hagar's visitor is called 'the angel of the LORD' (four times), and he is also called *Yahweh* and *Elohim*, the all-seeing God. The identification is beyond dispute.

Jacob also refers to this angel as God (Gen. 48). In his last days, Jacob prays for God's blessing on the sons of Joseph (Ephraim and Manasseh). He refers to Jehovah as God (*Elohim*) and Angel (*malach*). 'May the God before whom my fathers Abraham and Isaac walked, the God who has been my shepherd all my life to this day, the Angel who has delivered me from all harm — may he bless these boys' (Gen. 48:15–16). The definite article is used each time (the God, the Angel). Jacob is praying to the angel of God who is God. In other words the Bible tells us that God himself is sometimes designated by the term *malach* (angel or messenger).

In Genesis 31 Jacob is again dealing with the 'angel of God': 'Then the angel of God said to me in the dream ... I am the God of Bethel, where you anointed a pillar and where you made a vow to me' (Gen. 31:11,13). Bethel means 'house of God'. Jacob had changed its name from Luz to Bethel because God met with him there (Gen. 28). The God of Bethel specifically identified himself as *Yahweh Elohim*, the God of Abraham and Isaac (Gen. 28:13). This is 'Exhibit B' proving that 'God' and 'angel' are both titles belonging to Jehovah and that 'the angel of God' (also known as 'the angel of the LORD') is none other than the God of Bethel himself.

Similarly, the angel of the LORD who spoke with Gideon is God (Judg. 6). When this great personage spoke to Gideon he was first called 'the angel of the LORD' (6:12). After Gideon's reply, the same angel is called '*Yahweh*' (The LORD): 'The LORD (יְהוָה) turned to him and said, "Go in the strength you have and save Israel out of Midian's hand"' (6:14). As Gideon continued speaking to this personage (whom the inspired writer calls both 'Jehovah' and 'the angel of Jehovah'), he addressed him by the polite and respectful title 'Lord' (אֲדֹנָי, *Adonai*). This was presumably due to the fact that Gideon was not yet sure who he was. As the dialogue continued, the visitor is again called '*Yahweh*' (the LORD) in verse 16.

Gideon now realizes that this is not just an angel. It dawns on him that this could be the awesome 'angel of the LORD'. Gideon would have heard about him, the one who had appeared to Hagar, Abraham, Jacob and, more recently, Joshua. Gideon wondered if he was seeing this same exalted visitor. So he said, 'give me a sign that it is really you talking with me' (6:17). Gideon is particularizing it. Is it *you*? Are you the one known to our fathers as 'the angel of the LORD'?

All together the writer uses three different names for this mysterious personage. In Judges 6:16 he is called '*Yahweh*': 'The LORD (*Yahweh*) answered, "I will be with you."' But the next time that we see him speaking (6:20) he is called 'the angel of God' (*malach Elohim*). Then twice in verse 21 he is called 'the angel of the LORD'. Regardless of what Gideon knows or thinks, the inspired writer tells us repeatedly and unambiguously that the person speaking to Gideon is *Yahweh*, who is also called the angel of *Yahweh* and the angel of God.

After Gideon's sacrifices and offerings were consumed by fire springing out of the rock the reality hit him with that characteristic fear of the divine presence: 'When Gideon realized that it was the angel of the LORD, he exclaimed, "Ah, Sovereign Lord! I have seen the angel of the LORD face to face!" But the LORD (*Yahweh*) said to him, "Peace! Do not be afraid. You are not going to die." So Gideon built an altar to the LORD (*Yahweh*) there and called it The LORD is Peace (*Yahweh Shalom*)' (6:22–24).

Significantly, he did not name it 'The angel of the LORD is Peace', although up until now that is all he knew his visitor to be. This is 'Exhibit C' proving that the Old Testament regards the following terms as interchangeable: angel of Jehovah, Jehovah, angel of God, and the God of Bethel. We have seen sufficient proof of the fact that the 'angel of the LORD' in the Old Testament is a theophany — the appearance of almighty God himself.[1]

He is God-sent

We return to the question noted earlier. If the angel of the LORD is the LORD, then why bother to call him an angel? What is the point of changing God's name from *God* who sends to *messenger* who is sent? How can God be both the sender and the sent? Frankly, he cannot if he is only one person. But Scripture makes it clear that God is triune.

God is Father, Son and Holy Spirit, a Godhead of three equal persons. This means that if the Father sends the Son, or if the Son sends the Holy Spirit, the one who comes is both *God* and *God-sent*. He is both God and God's messenger. It is possible for God to send and be sent. It is possible to be 'the LORD' and 'the messenger of the LORD'. So all this Old Testament teaching on the angel of the LORD is preparing us for the doctrine of the trinity. It tells us over and over again that in God there is both unity and plurality. There is unity because there is only one God (*Yahweh*) but within the one divine being there is plurality, three divine persons. In perfect accord with this is the New Testament teaching that while Jesus is God in all his fullness (Col. 2:9), he is also God-sent, the messenger of God. There is nothing new in this. It continues a well-established theme in the Old Testament as we have just seen.

It is not surprising then that the strongest opposition to these biblical truths comes from those who deny the doctrine of the trinity: the Arian cults like The Watchtower Society and other Unitarians. They strenuously deny that the angel of the LORD is the LORD. To them it is impossible to understand how one individual can be both 'God' and 'sent from God'. So they employ many rationalizations to explain away the extensive evidence that proves this truth.

One way of doing this is to resort to the literary device called 'metonymy' (using the name of one thing for something associated with it), like the 'White House' for the president or 'the circumcision' for Jews. Thus all the references to the deity of the angel of the LORD are categorized as metonymy where angel of the LORD merely signifies the LORD. But the argument is completely barren. That is not how metonymy is used. Neither inside nor outside the Bible does the representative of a high authority claim that 'I am that authority'. Certainly there is no instance of any mere representative of God claiming to actually be God. But the angel of the LORD does make that claim. When he spoke to Moses in the burning bush, he said, 'I am the God of Abraham and of Isaac and of Jacob' (Exod. 3:2–6). We are not talking here of mere metonymy but of literal equality. This is not representation but identification. This is not merely associating two things together: it is equating them. The two are one and the same, almighty God!

But remember, God is not a man. When God revealed himself in human form, he was condescending to our frailty and limitations. God met with men in the least frightening way, walking, talking, eating and drinking with them like a man. In a sense, there was a great risk involved here because men might then conclude that God was a man. Men might assume that the material 'messenger form' in which he chose to appear was essentially and naturally his. So it was necessary for God to also convey his infinite spiritual nature. How was this done? The angel, who was God, also spoke of the God who sent him. He still referred to God as 'another', a person he knew and related to. Behind the *sent God* is the *sending God*. Behind the God who spoke as a visible messenger there was always the invisible God who sent the messenger.

There is still a deep and unsearchable 'unknown' about God even when he reveals himself. Indeed it is *as* God reveals himself and *because* he reveals himself that we come to sense his deep and unsearchable greatness (the incomprehensibility of God). We know him truly but not fully. We know him reliably but not analytically. God delights to make himself known to us as he really is. But that has big implications. It means that he is revealing to us the infinite, eternal, immense, invisible and unchanging pure Spirit, the all knowing, all powerful everlasting one who exists before all space and time, who transcends and who governs all space and time.

Paradoxically for us then, the more we know about God the more obvious are the gaps in our knowledge. The closer we draw to the knowledge of infinity, the further away it is. There is something absolutely unmanageable about God. He is awesome, great, unique, incomparable, intimidating and different from anything and everything. There are no examples or illustrations of God. That is why in all these appearances of God as the angel of the LORD the eyewitnesses sensed the 'hidden God' behind the 'revealed God'. Behind this 'man', behind this 'angel', there was a profound and mysterious reality that invariably brought them to feel that they would die. All this is absolutely essential to a right doctrine of God. There is always an immeasurable distance between the Creator and creation, the infinite and the finite.

All of this points to Christ. He is the ultimate *God-sent God*. He is God with us in visible human form. There was nothing in his appearance to mark him out from an average Jewish man of his age. But those who knew him best realized how much more there was to Jesus. 'Who is this? Even the winds and the waves obey him?' (Mark 4:41). They were struggling with the infinite and invisible God who has no material form, now appearing in finite, visible human form.

Let us be thankful for the true revelations of God in human form in the Old Testament and New Testament. Let us never be distant from the God who came so close, but let us never be so familiar with God that we ignore his lofty throne. Every attempt to remove the ultimate mystery from God is from the devil. To God be all the glory.

QUESTIONS FOR DISCUSSION

1. *What important truth about God is stressed in Deuteronomy 6:4; 1 Corinthians 8:4–6 and 1 Thessalonians 1:8–9?*

2. *How is the doctrine of the trinity made inevitable by Matthew 28:18–19; Luke 1:35; Luke 3:21–22; John 1:1–14 and 2 Corinthians 13:14?*

3. *How does John 14:30; Acts 5:3–4 and Ephesians 4:30 prove that the Holy Spirit is a divine person not just divine power?*

THE GUIDE

CHAPTER FOUR

CHRIST: THE ANGEL OF THE LORD

BIBLE READING

Exodus 3:1-15

We have seen that 'the angel of the LORD' is a theophany (an appearance of God). He is in fact a Christophany (an appearance of Christ). He is Christ appearing in the Old Testament period before his incarnation in the womb of the virgin Mary. The angel of the LORD who met with Hagar, Abraham, Moses, Jacob, Gideon and Manoah was God the Son, the second person of the trinity. This is not claiming that he appeared in the same form as the man Jesus of Nazareth. Rather he appeared in a temporary human form to guide and bless his people.

The evidence for this is not as direct and explicit as is the evidence for his deity. Therefore, our conclusions should be cautious rather than overly dogmatic. However, although indirect, the reasons are sound and not easily dismissed. The evidence is in the nature of deductions and logical consequences arising from various identical properties shared by the angel of the LORD and Christ the Son of God. Three identities especially deserve our thoughtful attention.

1. Identity of functions
2. Identity of names
3. Identity of testaments

Identity of functions

Christ the Son of God and the angel of the LORD perform identical functions. There is a significant coincidence of truths about them. These are hard to explain in any other way except that they are one and the same person. Their functional identity is seen in three ways. Each one is God appearing in human form, each appears at key points in the covenant and each one functions as the God-sent God.

God appears in human form

Since the angel of the LORD is God in human form, it raises a question. Does the New Testament develop this 'God appearing as a man' theme? The answer is *yes* — in fact that is what the New Testament is all about! In the Old Testament 'God appearing in human form' is just one of many themes, but in the New Testament it is *the* theme! The advent of the Son of God in human form is the central issue and preoccupation of the message, the theme of all themes. So already the equation between the angel of the LORD and God the Son is being drawn.

God appears at key points

As we noted in previous chapters, the angel of the LORD

appeared at key points in covenant history. He came to distinguish Abraham's *naturally* begotten son (Ishmael) from Abraham's *miraculously* begotten son (Isaac). He came to redeem Abraham and his posterity. He controlled the events when faithful Abraham was prepared to sacrifice his only son, but God provided an innocent substitute so that Isaac could live. He came rebuking Israel for sin. He came to deliver Israel from her enemies. These were all key points of covenant activity. What the angel of the LORD did each time was critical for the church.

The New Testament describes *the* key point in all of history: the coming of Christ. This New Testament event is variously described as 'the fullness of time', 'the right time' and 'the consummation of the ages'. Where then is the angel of the LORD who appeared over and over again at key points in history? If ever we would expect to see him it would be now! This is history's climax! All the prophets yearned for this day. Has he disappeared from the stage when the most important act is being played out?

Of course not! Not only does he appear again but in a greater and more significant way than ever before. Christ is the angel of the LORD. He is *Immanuel*, God with us, just as the angel of the LORD was God with us but now in an even greater sense. Everything rests on his shoulders. Here is the day that Abraham rejoiced to see. If this is not so, how do we account for the absence of God's messenger at the greatest point of covenant history?

God and God-sent

We have seen the proof that the angel of the LORD is both God and God-sent. He consistently speaks and acts as God and assumes the prerogatives of deity. He accepts divine names such as the 'God who sees' and 'Yahweh'. He accepts the worship of people who characteristically feared for their life having seen him as God. Yet being God he still speaks of God as 'another', a distinct person whom he knows and who sent him and whose messenger he is. So the angel of the LORD was quite conscious of being both God and God's messenger. This raises a question.

THINK ABOUT IT

Does the New Testament develop and enlarge on this theme? Does it present us with any equivalent character who is both God and God-sent? Does any New Testament person speak of God in both the first person (*I Am*) and the third person (*He is*)? Does any man legitimately claim to be the same as God in all respects? Yes, of course, it is Christ Jesus!

Many texts show us that Jesus was sent from God, for example, John 14:24: 'These words you hear are not my own; they belong to the Father who sent me.' Other texts tell us that Jesus is God: 'I and the Father are one' and 'Anyone who has seen me has seen the Father' (John 10:30 and 14:9). He speaks as the eternal and everlasting God: 'Before Abraham was born, I am' (John 8:58). The New Testament gives clear testimony to the deity of Christ: 'For in Christ all the fullness of the Deity lives in bodily form' (Col. 2:9). 'In the beginning was the Word, and the Word was with God, and the Word was God' (John 1:1).

We cannot escape the fact that Jesus claimed to be both God and God-sent: 'For this reason the Jews tried all the harder to kill him ... he was even calling God his own Father, making himself equal with God' (John 5:18).

Therefore, there is an exact identity of functions between Christ and the angel of the LORD. This is very pointed as far as *redemption* is concerned. Remember how Jacob prayed to God: 'The God before whom my fathers Abraham and Isaac walked, The God who has been my shepherd all my life to this day, The angel who has redeemed me from all evil, bless the lads' (Gen. 48:15–16, NASB). Who is the only redeemer? Surely no one needs proof that it is Christ! Over and over again he is identified as the Redeemer: 'In him we have redemption through his blood' (Eph. 1:7). Jacob's redeemer is our redeemer, Christ the Messiah, the Son of God. Thus Christ is the angel of the LORD.

Identity of names

It is no mere coincidence that both Christ and the angel of the LORD share the names 'Mighty God', 'Wonderful' and 'I am'.

'Mighty God'

The two main terms for 'Mighty God' in the Hebrew Bible are *El Gibbor* (אֵל גִּבּוֹר) and 'Lord God Almighty' (יהוה אֱלֹהֵי הַצְּבָאוֹת) or, literally, 'Lord God of Hosts'. Isaiah used the term *El Gibbor* for Christ in his famous prophecy: 'For to us a child is born, to us a son is given, and the government will be on his shoulders. And he will be called Wonderful Counselor, *Mighty God* ' (Isa. 9:6).[1]

Hosea called the angel of the LORD the 'Mighty God' using the other equivalent term ('LORD God Almighty'). He was describing what happened at Bethel when Jacob wrestled with the divine messenger: 'He struggled with the angel and overcame him; he wept and begged for his favour. He found him at Bethel and talked with him there — the LORD God Almighty, the LORD is his name of renown!' (Hosea 12:4–5). So, if Christ is the 'Mighty God' and the angel of the LORD is the 'Mighty God' we are constrained to conclude that it is the same person.

'Wonderful'

This name is used of Christ in Isaiah 9:6 (NASB): 'He will be called wonderful' (פֶּלֶא). Isaiah actually uses the noun here not the adjective: 'He will be called Wonder', which also implies that he is wonderful.

Compare this with Judges 13:18 where Manoah asks the angel of the LORD to state his name. He replied, 'Why do you ask my name, seeing it is wonderful?' (NASB) (פֶּלִאי). It is the same Hebrew word used by Isaiah only now it is in its adjectival form. In both cases it denotes mystery, something too profound for men to grasp. Therefore, when the Bible refers to two characters, calling them both 'Mighty God' and expressing the same sense of awe and mystery about them (wonder), what can we conclude? Surely they are one and the same person!

'I am'

It is important to know that God's name, *Yahweh*, is a form of the Hebrew verb 'to be' (היה). When God tells us that his name is *Yahweh* he tells us that his name is 'I am'. It expresses his eternal and unchangeable nature. This is the idea behind the many 'I am' statements of Jesus: I am the bread of life; I am the light of the world; I am the good shepherd; I am the resurrection; I am the way, the truth and the life; and before Abraham was I am.

This last case is very pointed. The Jews were upset that Jesus claimed to be so great, so they said to him, 'Are you greater than our father Abraham? ... Who do you think you are? ... You are not yet fifty years old ... and you have seen Abraham!' (John 8:53,57). His answer was emphatic: 'I tell you the truth ... before Abraham was born, I am!' (John 8:58). Jesus is claiming to be the ageless and eternal one, the same yesterday, today and forever. He is the Ancient of Days, who was, and is, and is to come! It is a potent claim to deity. What is his connection with the angel of the LORD? We must think back to the burning bush.

When God met Moses at the burning bush he appeared as 'the angel of the LORD'. The text says, 'There the angel of the LORD appeared to him in flames of fire from within a bush' (Exod. 3:2). But the one in the midst of the bush was God: 'God called to him from within the bush' (Exod. 3:4). When Moses asked about his name, 'God said to Moses, "I AM WHO I AM. This is what you are to say to the Israelites: 'I AM has sent me to you'"' (Exod. 3:14). This is the connection! If the angel of the LORD is the eternal 'I AM', and if Christ Jesus is the eternal 'I AM' then Christ *is* the angel of the LORD!

Identity of testaments

There is an essential unity in the Old and New Testaments. The old predicts, hopes and waits for the new. The new fulfils, develops and explains the old. Where does the Old Testament end and the New Testament start? The connecting point is the book of the prophet Malachi. His name means 'my messenger' or 'my angel'. He promised that God would send two more 'angels/messengers': '"See, I will send my messenger, who will prepare the way before me. Then suddenly the Lord you are seeking will come to his temple; the messenger of the covenant, whom you desire, will come," says the LORD Almighty' (Mal. 3:1).

The first 'angel/messenger' is also figuratively described as Elijah: 'Behold, I am going to send you Elijah the prophet before the coming of the great and terrible day of the LORD' (Mal. 4:5, NASB). He prepares the way for the second and greater 'angel/messenger of the covenant' who will cleanse and purify God's people. His advent is 'the great and terrible day of the LORD'. It is clear from the New Testament that the first messenger refers to John the Baptist (see Matt. 11:10–14; Mark 1:2–4; Luke 1:76; 7:27). The second figure ('angel of the covenant') must refer to Christ, whose way John prepared. This is in line with his description in Malachi as the LORD coming to his temple for the purposes of purification and judgement (Mal. 3–4).

Jesus put the matter beyond doubt:

> For all the Prophets and the Law prophesied until John. And if you are willing to accept it, he is the Elijah who was to come... But I tell you, Elijah has already come, and they did not recognize him, but have done to him everything they wished... Then the disciples understood that he was talking to them about John the Baptist (Matt. 11:13–14; 17:12–13).[2]

This is the identity of testaments. The Old Testament ends with the promise of the angel of the LORD, and the New Testament begins with its fulfilment. This is good evidence for interpreting Christ as the angel of the LORD.

REMEMBER THIS

Christ appeared in the Old Testament but not as Jesus of Nazareth. There is a distinction between Christophany and the Incarnation. Jesus of Nazareth was never seen until the virgin birth. When Christ appeared as the angel of the LORD in the Old Testament, it was purely an 'appearance'. It was a temporary human form. He appeared as a man but he did not actually become a man (just as the Holy Spirit appeared as a dove without actually becoming a dove). *The human form seen by Hagar, Abraham and Gideon was not the human form born from Mary's womb.* We must be careful. To say that 'Christ is the angel of the LORD' does not mean that he was incarnate at Bethel before being incarnate at Bethlehem.

Remember also that whenever God appears in history his words are more important than his physical appearance. The Bible pays little attention to the physical appearance of Jesus and the angel of the LORD. In each case it is his words and works that should occupy all of our interest and study. He speaks as our God, our Maker, our Creator, our Judge and our only hope in life and death. He is prominent at key points throughout history. *Is he prominent in your life?* He is found in both testaments. *Is he found in your heart?* This is the big issue. May we love and serve him all of our days.

QUESTIONS FOR DISCUSSION

1. What is the explicit and implicit evidence that Jesus is God in John 5:19–23; John 20:19–22,28–29 and Hebrews 1:1–6?

2. How do the following texts show the ongoing importance of 'theophany' in Christian doctrine? (See Gen. 3:8; Exod. 13:21,24; Num. 14:14; Matt. 5:8; 1 Thess. 4:16.)

3. Identify the particular features of God incarnate being stressed in 1 Timothy 3:16; Philippians 2:5–11; Hebrews 1:8–12 and Revelation 1:10–20.

THE GUIDE

CHAPTER FIVE

AN OLD SOLDIER AND AN OXGOAD

BIBLE READING

Judges 3:7–11,31

An old soldier and an oxgoad were two of the instruments used by Almighty God to save Israel from its enemies. The old soldier was Othniel, the first in the line of judges named in this book. The oxgoad refers to Shamgar, the third judge. He was an unlikely saviour with an unlikely weapon. In between them comes Ehud whom we will consider separately. Othniel and Shamgar provide some valuable lessons for us.

Othniel: the old soldier

As we noted in chapter one, the book of Judges is structured around a recurring four-part cycle: the Israelites sin, God strengthens their enemies, the Israelites cry to God and God provides a deliverer (judge) to save them. The writer announces the first two parts of the cycle: 'The Israelites did evil in the eyes of the LORD; they forgot the LORD their God and served the Baals and the Asherahs' (3:7). So God strengthened their enemies, the Mesopotamians: 'The anger of the LORD burned against Israel so that he sold them into the hands of Cushan-Rishathaim king of Aram Naharaim, to whom the Israelites were subject for eight years' (3:8).

The king's name is Cushan, with 'Rishathaim' (meaning double wickedness) added on. It is probably a nickname describing his nature, a very obnoxious, cruel and godless man. The eight years of subjection to him must have been terrible as Israel felt his oppressive grip. The rest of the cycle is described in verse 9: 'But when they cried out to the LORD, he raised up for them a deliverer, Othniel son of Kenaz, Caleb's younger brother, who saved them.'

Othniel's name means 'lion of God'. He had a privileged family tree. He was related to the godly Caleb by birth, Caleb was his uncle (3:9), and also by marriage, he married Caleb's daughter Acsah. You can read the story in Joshua 15 and Judges 1:11–15. Caleb wanted his daughter to marry a godly man of courage and faith. So he put out a challenge for any brave man to capture the city of Debir (also known as Kiriath Sepher). It was populated by the descendants of Anak who were unusually big people, giants called 'Anakim'.[1] Caleb promised his daughter in marriage to the successful man. That man was Othniel.

Courage was an evident quality in Othniel's family. Not only did he prove himself a brave soldier, but he also married a girl whose father, Caleb, was famous for courage and faith. Of the ten spies sent to report on the promised land, all except Joshua and Caleb were frightened by the giants who lived there. They were the only two left alive after Israel's forty years of wandering.

God records his high opinion of Caleb: '... he has followed the LORD fully' (Deut. 1:36, NASB).

All of his life Othniel had had the great privilege of being in a family nurtured by godly habits of trust, courage, obedience and steadfastness in the truth. He also married a girl who grew up with the same principles. The Lord had been preparing this saviour for Israel, one who was not afraid of either doubly big men (Anakim) or doubly wicked ones (King Cushan).

We also perceive that he was an old soldier. When Othniel delivered Israel he was an old man, well past the years of battle. The calculation starts with what we know of his uncle. Caleb tells us that he was forty years old when he spied out the promised land: 'I was forty years old when Moses the servant of the LORD sent me from Kadesh Barnea to explore the land. And I brought him back a report according to my convictions' (Josh. 14:7). Forty-five years later he remarked, 'Now then, just as the LORD promised, he has kept me alive for forty-five years since ... while Israel moved about in the desert. So here I am today, eighty-five years old! I am still as strong today as the day Moses sent me out; I'm just as vigorous to go out to battle now as I was then' (Josh. 14:10–11). This was a tough family: Caleb was still ready to fight at eighty-five! Now we can make some deductions about his nephew Othniel.

We know that he could not have been more than nineteen when his uncle spied out the land because the entire generation who were over twenty years of age died in the wilderness (except Moses, Joshua and Caleb). Start with an age of between one and nineteen, add forty-five years to the time described in Joshua 14 and add another thirty years to reach the time described in Judges 3. This means that Othniel was between seventy-six and ninety-four years old when God appointed him as the first judge-deliverer of Israel. That is hardly the age at which new recruits are taken into an army! He was an old soldier!

THINK ABOUT IT

Old age does not prevent God from using us in his kingdom work. Even if we are not fit and well like Othniel the principle still applies. If we are godly, courageous and faithful the Lord can and does use us to glorify his name, not in exactly the same way as Othniel but in numerous other ways. The general principle for old saints is seen in Psalm 92:14: 'They will still bear fruit in old age, they will stay fresh and green.'

Shamgar and the oxgoad

In Judges 3:31 we read, 'After Ehud came Shamgar son of Anath, who struck down six hundred Philistines with an oxgoad. He too saved Israel.' It is easy to quickly read and dismiss the little we do know about this man of God. He is only mentioned in this one verse. He is an unlikely saviour. His circumstances are very different from Othniel's. It seems that Shamgar did not have the privileged upbringing of a godly home. To begin with, Shamgar is not a Hebrew name but a Canaanite name. Also, his father (Anath) has the name of a Canaanite goddess — the female idol of sex and war. Apparently Shamgar came from one of the Hebrew families in the thick of the very apostasy responsible for their present trials and sufferings. His family was thoroughly pagan, adopting the ways and habits of Canaan, even its names and religions. If ever a man was an unlikely judge to deliver Israel it was Shamgar.

He used an unlikely weapon. Shamgar was probably a very poor man, a peasant, judging by his weapon and his skill in using it. An oxgoad was a large hardwood stick between eight and ten feet long. Farmers used such goads to control a team of oxen pulling a plough. The thick end, about six inches in diameter, bore a metal spike to stick into the oxen, making a team pull evenly. The smaller end normally had a blade for cleaning the plough. Anyone who drove oxen for a living had to be robust. Strong wrists, arms, and legs were needed to use the goad in one hand while controlling a plough with the other.

Obviously the oxgoad was not a conventional military weapon, but it would be quite a formidable thing in the hands of an experienced man. The Australian description of Shamgar the farmer is 'stocky as a Mallee bull'. To have met him in battle with his oxgoad in hand would have been unforgettable. Anyone who has witnessed Japanese stick-fighters performing will know the sort of damage that Shamgar could have inflicted. The very fact that it was an unlikely weapon could explain why he chose to use it. The Philistines would not have had their suspicions aroused by such a common everyday sight as a Hebrew peasant carrying an oxgoad. But the sight of an Israelite carrying a sword and shield was bound to draw attention.

Shamgar was a brave man and a skilled fighter. You would need to be brave to take on 600 Philistines armed only with a stick. Few would want to try it armed with a rifle! Even if he did not face the 600 Philistines all at one time (it probably refers to the total he struck down over a period) it was still a very courageous and formidable task. There would have been occasions when he was outnumbered, and after the first hundred or more were killed he would have been a marked man.

Shamgar did not let his lack of privileges prevent him from doing great work for God. Neither should we. He was faithful despite his ungodly family background and his poor peasant status. Within the Christian church there will always be a mixture of Othniels and Shamgars. Some are privileged to be born and bred in the church, being raised in godly ways. Paul acknowledged that this was true for Timothy: 'I have been reminded of your sincere faith, which first lived in your grandmother Lois and in your mother Eunice and, I am persuaded, now lives in you also' (2 Tim. 1:5).

But God also has his hand on others who come from ungodly homes. Real fighters and soldiers can come from both contexts. God uses them both. If you come from a good Christian home, thank God for the privilege. Follow the good example of faith in your mum and dad! Or if you come from a pagan home, be encouraged as you look at Shamgar. Some wonderful Christians have come from ungodly homes. They are real fighters for the truth. They know the bitter fruits of godlessness and will fight it against all comers without fear or favour. It is very encouraging to know that God uses all types of people.

THINK ABOUT IT

You must never think that you are not the right 'type' for God to use in his kingdom. God has no stereotyped servants. He uses a great variety of people, as different as Othniel and Shamgar. Indeed, the list of judges shows a large range of people whose differences are quite surprising. You must never say that, 'I'm not the sort of person God uses; I'm not very clever or very gifted; I'm not from a longstanding Christian family; I'm not very educated or I'm a bit of a rough diamond.' God requires faithfulness, and if that is genuine he can and will use you.

Paul writes, 'Now it is required that those who have been given a trust must prove faithful' (1 Cor. 4:2). Most of us will not be used in a spectacular way like the judges, but we will be used. The Lord notes every little act of faith, whether it is visiting a lonely believer or giving a glass of cold water in love. And *never* think that you are too old to serve! Who knows what the final results of an old saint's faithful witness will be?

We should always be conscious that the power is God's. The book of Judges is not a parade of heroic power brokers or larger-than-life ideal people. Like us, they all had their strengths and weaknesses: *Hearts of iron, feet of clay.*[2] Whatever strengths they had the fact is that their successes and victories were due to the power of God. For instance, regarding Othniel we read, 'The Spirit of the LORD came upon him, so that he became Israel's judge and went to war' (3:10). Although it is not said of every judge, it is said sufficiently often to make it clear that the judges were divinely empowered instruments. Other instances include the following:

- 'Then the Spirit of the LORD came upon Gideon' (6:34)
- 'Then the Spirit of the LORD came upon Jephthah... and from there he advanced against the Ammonites' (11:29)
- 'The Spirit of the LORD began to stir him [Samson]' (13:25)
- 'The Spirit of the LORD came upon him in power so that he tore the lion apart with his bare hands' (14:6)
- 'Then the Spirit of the LORD came upon him in power. He went down to Ashkelon, struck down

thirty of their men ...' (14:19)
- 'The Spirit of the LORD came upon him in power. The ropes on his arms became like charred flax, and the bindings dropped from his hands' (15:14)

The writer makes it plain repeatedly that he is not extolling the virtues and powers of men. He is recording the mighty works of God. The book of Judges illustrates the general principle by applying it to all God's covenant works: '"Not by might nor by power, but by my Spirit," says the LORD Almighty' (Zech. 4:6). This book, like every book in the Bible, is far more than history. It is covenant history. It depicts the God of history in complete control of all events so that his covenant purposes in the Messiah will stand. When Israel sinned, God raised up chastening foes then he sent delivering judges. Equipped by the Holy Spirit, the judges kept the covenant community from self-destructing so that the Messiah would come at the fullness of time.

This book gives a very clear picture of the sovereign God controlling all of history according to his will and purpose. He prospers whom he wills, strengthens whom he wills, counsels whom he wills, hardens whom he wills and has mercy on whom he wills. None of this denies the free and responsible actions of human beings. The actions of Israel and Mesopotamia and Othniel and Caleb were free and responsible.

The same is true for Shamgar and the Philistines and Moab and every human being. They all do what they want to do, but God rules and over-rules. The *Westminster Shorter Catechism* sums it up well: 'What are God's works of providence? God's works of providence are, his most holy, wise, and powerful preserving and governing all his creatures and all their actions' (*Westminster Shorter Catechism*, question 11).

We have the privilege of a greater task than the judges. The Holy Spirit equipped the judges and made them capable of extraordinary results. However, it is easy to sit back and marvel while failing to recognize the greater truth, that every Christian has the fullness of the Holy Spirit. Every Christian has the abiding and indwelling Holy Spirit of God. We have the means of doing greater things than Othniel, Shamgar and the judges. They were enabled to *destroy* large numbers of God's enemies. We are enabled and commanded to *convert* them and to make them members of the church. By preaching the gospel of Jesus Christ we are privileged to witness many lives being reconciled from enemies to friends.

We know that God is 'able to do immeasurably more than all we ask or imagine, according to his power that is at work within us' (Eph. 3:20). If you love Christ you do have the Holy Spirit, and you are exactly the person that God delights to use. Whether you are 'an old soldier' or your resources are limited to an oxgoad, use all that you have for the glory of God. 'Whatever you do, work at it with all your heart, as working for the Lord' (Col. 3:23).

QUESTIONS FOR DISCUSSION

1. In what sense does Christ enable his disciples to do greater works than he did? (See John 14:12.)

2. Do all true Christians have the fullness of the Holy Spirit? (See John 3:34; 7:37–39; Eph. 1:3; 5:1; Col. 2:10; 2 Peter 1:3.)

3. According to Hebrews 11:32–39 the main characteristic of the judges was 'faith'. What exactly does this mean?

THE GUIDE

CHAPTER SIX

A POINTED MESSAGE FROM GOD

LOOK IT UP

BIBLE READING

Judges 3:12–30

INTRODUCTION

As soon as Othniel died, Israel went back to her old godless ways (3:11–12). The forty years of peace were over. God raised up a new enemy to chastise them, Moab on the eastern front. Helped by the Ammonites and Amalekites, king Eglon defeated Israel and took possession of Jericho 'the city of the palm trees'.[1] Eglon oppressed Israel for eighteen years. Again they cried to the Lord and again they received mercy. God raised up a new judge to deliver them, Ehud the Benjamite.

Ehud must have been a reliable man because he was in charge of taking the 'tribute' to Eglon (3:15). These were the taxes imposed by a conquering nation on its victims for sparing their lives. They consisted of gold, silver, fabrics, spices and foods. It was important to choose a trustworthy person to deliver these tributes because the people would suffer greatly if he did not get the job done.

The writer had good reason to inform us that Ehud was left-handed. This is not a problem in our culture but in those days it was considered to be a handicap. This is reflected in the Hebrew text where the word for left-handed means literally 'hindered in the right hand' (אִטֵּר יַד־יְמִינוֹ). It is also reflected in the Latin word *sinister* and the French word *gauche*, both meaning awkward or left-handed. To be left-handed was seen as being defective, being weaker and less able than right-handed people.[2] The story actually hangs on this detail. Ehud turned his assumed disadvantage into an advantage. He got close to the king of Moab, who would not suspect a sword being drawn on him by a left-hander, and he delivered a very pointed message from God. We read:

> Now Ehud had made a double-edged sword about a foot and a half long, which he strapped to his right thigh under his clothing. He presented the tribute to Eglon king of Moab, who was a very fat man. After Ehud had presented the tribute, he sent on their way the men who had carried it. At the idols near Gilgal he himself turned back and said, 'I have a secret message for you, O king.' The king said, 'Quiet!' And all his attendants left him. Ehud then approached him while he was sitting alone in the upper room of his summer palace and said, 'I have a message from God for you.' As the king rose from his seat, Ehud reached with his left hand, drew the sword from his right thigh and plunged it into the king's belly. Even the handle sank in after the blade, which came out his back. Ehud did not pull the sword out, and the fat closed in over it. Then Ehud went out to the porch; he shut the

doors of the upper room behind him and locked them. After he had gone, the servants came and found the doors of the upper room locked. They said, 'He must be relieving himself in the inner room of the house.' They waited to the point of embarrassment, but when he did not open the doors of the room, they took a key and unlocked them. There they saw their lord fallen to the floor, dead. While they waited, Ehud got away (3:16–26).

Three considerations will help us understand this episode in salvation history:

1. The events: what actually happened here?
2. The ethics: how are we to evaluate this gory episode?
3. The edification: what practical lessons are appropriate?

The events

The map at right will help to clarify these events. Ehud led the couriers delivering the tribute to the Moabite king at Jericho, 'the city of palms'. Eglon had set up his command post there in the land of Israel. 'After Ehud had presented the tribute, he sent on their way the men who had carried it. At the idols near Gilgal he himself

A POINTED MESSAGE FROM GOD 83

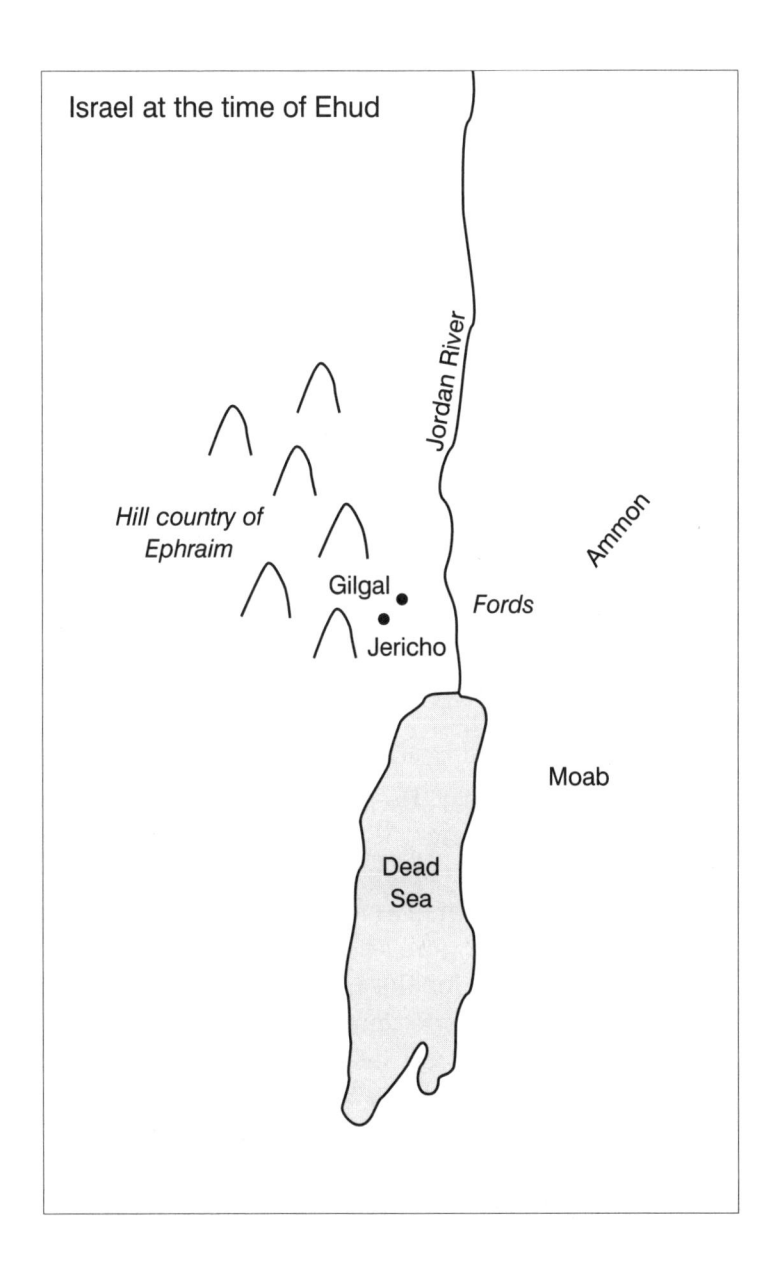

Israel at the time of Ehud

Hill country of Ephraim

Gilgal

Jericho

Jordan River

Fords

Ammon

Moab

Dead Sea

turned back and said, "I have a secret message for you, O king"' (3:18–19).

This means that the whole party (including Ehud) continued further east, from Jericho to Gilgal, where the Moabites had erected stone idols to reinforce their superiority over Israel. Gilgal was where Joshua had made the stone monument after crossing the Jordan. But before they reached Gilgal, Ehud parted company with the others and returned to Jericho alone to arrange a private meeting with king Eglon. This was shrewd. Having paid the tribute first there were no indications of imminent rebellion. Eglon had no reason to be suspicious of this lone left-handed Israelite.

After killing king Eglon, Ehud escaped and summoned his army to finish the task of defeating Moab:

> Ehud got away. He passed by the idols and escaped to Seirah. When he arrived there, he blew a trumpet in the hill country of Ephraim, and the Israelites went down with him from the hills, with him leading them. 'Follow me,' he ordered, 'for the LORD has given Moab, your enemy, into your hands' (3:26–28).

It was successful. Israel blocked off the fords (shallow crossings) on the Jordan River east of Gilgal. This meant that none could escape and no new reinforcements from Moab could enter Israel:

So they followed him down and, taking possession of the fords of the Jordan that led to Moab, they allowed no one to cross over. At that time they struck down about ten thousand Moabites, all vigorous and strong; not a man escaped. That day Moab was made subject to Israel, and the land had peace for eighty years (3:28–30).

There is an important background fact to keep in mind. Jericho was the first city that Joshua destroyed when God's people crossed into the promised land more than a century earlier. Joshua invoked a curse on anyone who rebuilt Jericho:

> Joshua pronounced this solemn oath: 'Cursed before the LORD is the man who undertakes to rebuild this city, Jericho: At the cost of his firstborn son will he lay its foundations; at the cost of his youngest will he set up its gates.' So the LORD was with Joshua, and his fame spread throughout the land (Josh. 6:26–27).

REMEMBER THIS

God will not be mocked! By ignoring that oath, Eglon openly defied God. He denied the word of God and despised the people of God. Like Pharaoh before him, Eglon had only contempt for *Yahweh* and his covenant and his people. He arrogantly assumed that he could ignore Joshua's warning with impunity. He was about to find out the hard way that it was no idle threat.

The ethics

How are we to evaluate Ehud's actions? Was he acting immorally here? Was he simply a deceitful murderer, a crafty assassin? Was this whole thing just another gory event that should never have happened? A lot of rash opinions have been expressed about this. Humanism and sentiment have protested, but our duty is to think biblically. A few observations will help us to do that.

Remember who Eglon was

Eglon was at war with God and God's people. He was an idol worshipper and a hardened denier of Jehovah. Eglon grew fatter at the expense of God's people, forcing them to fill his coffers with annual tributes. Whatever Israel's faults were they were still the people of God, and anyone who gets rich at their expense is provoking God to intervene.

Remember who Ehud was

Ehud was not a private person. He was God's agent, God's instrument, the judge (defender and saviour) of Israel. Ehud was the civil magistrate, the arm of the law. It was his duty to use the sword. God has assigned a punitive task to civil magistrates who must not bear the sword in vain (Rom. 13:4). Eglon had become a law unto himself, mocking God and robbing God's people, and Ehud's duty in delivering Israel was to bring strict justice to Eglon. Ehud acted in obedience to his God-given task as a judge, showing a special blend of courage, shrewdness and divine providence.

A common mistake occurs when people put Ehud on the same level as us. They draw the invalid equation that 'Ehud = every man', and then they conclude that he behaved unethically. Of course none of us has the right to assassinate a godless tyrant in the service of God. That is taking the law into our own hands. But Ehud's case is entirely different. God *had* placed the law into his hands! Ehud can neither be dismissed as a deceitful assassin nor copied as an example for us to follow. He is in a unique position as a unique officer in God's kingdom history. It would have been presumptuous for any ordinary Israelite to do what Ehud did. We should also notice a few features of his actions.

He spoke only the truth

At no time did Ehud lie to Eglon. When Ehud said, 'I have a secret message for you, O king' (3:19), he spoke the truth. It was not the entire truth, but the enemies of God have no right to the entire truth. Then Ehud stated it more specifically as, 'I have a message from God for you' (3:20), which was precisely the case — a very pointed message from God. All this reinforces Ehud's unique role. He was conscious of acting for God. It was not simply Ehud striking down Eglon: it was God striking down Eglon.

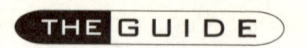

Did God tell him more?

There may well have been extra revelations given to Ehud, guiding him into this plan. Although they are not recorded in this book, it would be rash to deny the possibility. The likelihood of extra revelation is implied by Ehud's words to Israel in verse 28: "'Follow me,' he ordered, "for the LORD has given Moab, your enemy, into your hands.'" Ehud already knew the results. He had learned the mind of God. There is an extra dimension here compared with Othniel's case.

With Othniel we were simply told by the narrator that the Lord gave the enemy into his hand so that he prevailed (3:10). But Ehud *knew* it as a conscious fact before it happened! It seems that the Lord had told him to first strike down the king of Moab, the success of that risky plot signifying a subsequent greater victory over Moab. But whether there was extra revelation or not, there was no question about the divine will. God had already repeatedly and unambiguously commanded Israel to leave no survivors among these godless pagans. He had tolerated them for an extra 400 years, but now their time was up (see Deut. 12:2–3; 20:16–18; Num. 33:51–55).

Joshua had gotten the message

'He [Joshua] left no survivors. He totally destroyed all who breathed, just as the LORD, the God of

Israel, had commanded' (Josh. 10:40). Israel would not be in such a mess if they had followed Joshua. But they did not: 'The people served the LORD throughout the lifetime of Joshua ... after that ... another generation grew up, who knew neither the LORD nor what he had done for Israel. Then the Israelites did evil in the eyes of the LORD and served the Baals' (2:7,10–11). For all these reasons we should be very careful not to consign Ehud's disposal of Eglon to the 'unethical' bin.

The edification

Bible history is never written as a news bulletin. It is not mere information but is written to train and equip us for godly living. There is no point in merely knowing the details of Judges 3 without learning from it.

One thing we learn is that faith requires courage. Even those who criticize Ehud's methods are ready to admit his courage. He was prepared to risk his own life to deliver Israel from her enemies. When God declares his will on any matter let us get on with proper obedience, no matter what the cost.

We also learn that true faith is well planned. Ehud was careful and well organized. He did not just vaguely and generally set out to deliver Israel. He made up a detailed plan, set goals and targets and then pursued and achieved them. Ehud's plan included a clear aim to destroy the enemy, King Eglon. We can reconstruct his thoughts: How will I do this? I'll make a suitable weapon (and he did). I'll arrange to be 'alone' with him (and he did). I'll arrange my escape without giving alarm (so he locked the doors of the king's private room). I'll rally all Israel to block off the fords of the Jordan River (and he did).

Ehud was a shrewd and careful steward of his gifts and opportunities. The concealed sword, the opportunity grasped at tribute time and the strategic blocking of the fords are all evidences of this fact. Every plan for serving God involves certain risks. There are always unknown factors. Things might not work out as we thought, but a plan is still necessary. Ehud knew the risks of being alone with an enemy king in his stronghold: What if the sword was found on him? What if Eglon didn't dismiss all his servants? What if Eglon cried out at the critical moment, alerting all the guards?

REMEMBER THIS

We can learn a lesson from Ehud. Every good plan takes calculated risks. It leaves room for the sovereignty of God. Indeed a good plan consciously depends on God's over-ruling hand. The lesson repeated over and over again in Scripture is that leaders of the people of God need to set wise plans and goals that fit their contexts. How can the troops be encouraged to pursue them? How will they get the gospel out to the community? How will the church be faithful, relevant and edifying? Without a

> plan we just stay in a rut. We aim at nothing in particular, and we probably achieve exactly that — nothing in particular.

We also learn that unbelief is folly. God's enemies are doomed. One of the overwhelming lessons from Judges is that God's enemies can only prosper for the short time he allows them. But calamity will inevitably fall on them. It happened to Eglon and it will happen to all who resist God. Those who feel squeamish and balk at the awful circumstances of Eglon's death have no idea of the horrors of hell. Death by the stab of a sword is swift and easy compared with the second death. You must not think that when Eglon fell dead that his suffering was finally over. No, it had only just begun. Already his godless soul suffers torments, but when Christ returns for the day of judgement, Eglon will suffer the pains of hell in both body and soul forever, along with all who ignore God. Therefore, God warns us to treat hell seriously.

Terrible death is not epitomized in Eglon. Rather, look to Christ! The death of Christ was not only far worse physically, being suspended alive for hours on the spikes driven through his hands and feet, but the spiritual trauma was indescribably worse. Christ was innocent but Eglon was not. Eglon suffered for his own sins, Christ suffered for the sins of multitudes of others, too many to number. Eglon was merely a stained man, but Christ is God incarnate, perfect in righteousness. The implications of Calvary are far more profound than those of a million other deaths.

The message of the gospel is very pointed to those who enjoy much greater light than Eglon. Swift death and destruction will overtake every unbeliever. Do you know when God will snuff out your life? Will it be at the very moment when you have never felt better, like the rich fool? Will God have a left-handed message for you today (concealed, unexpected and out of the blue)? And if so, what will be the instrument? Will it be an automobile accident, a bolt of lightning, a terrible sickness or a heart attack?

How haughty to presume that we have no need to fear! Ignoring the issue will only provoke God. You enjoy a privilege right now that Eglon did not have. You can avoid the punitive judgement that all men deserve. You are reading a pointed message designed to save you. You now know that those who do not lovingly obey Christ are God's enemies. There is no neutral ground. You know that without faith your position is perilous!

Remember what Jesus said in Luke 13:1–5 when people reported some grim deaths, like the slaughter of Galileans by Pilate and eighteen people crushed by a falling tower. He gave them a pointed message. He warned them not to think that the victims were any worse than other people. Do not think that they were worse culprits. 'I tell you, no! But unless you repent, you too will all perish' (Luke 13:3). Never mind dwelling on the sword embedded deep into Eglon's stomach for unless you repent you will all likewise perish.

The pointed question for each of us is clear. Am I just another Eglon who will perish in judgement or do I stand with Jesus Christ? He is the final and great Judge. Is he for me or against me? Jesus says, 'Whoever believes in the Son has eternal life, but whoever rejects the Son will not see life, for God's wrath remains on him' (John 3:36). May we take these pointed lessons to heart, and by loving Christ may we discover that the sharp two-edged sword proceeding from his mouth is used for our blessing rather than our destruction.

QUESTIONS FOR DISCUSSION

1. What are the implications of Christ's instruction: 'be as shrewd as snakes and as innocent as doves' (Matt. 10:16)? See also Romans 12:2 and Psalm 119:97–105.

2. Read Matthew 25:14–30. How does the parable show our need for good planning?

3. What happens to the gospel if the doctrine of 'hell' is denied? (See Matt. 10:28; Mark 9:42–48; Luke 16:10–31; Rev. 20:10–15.)

THE GUIDE

CHAPTER SEVEN

BARAK AND DEBORAH IN CONCERT

BIBLE READING

Judges 4 and 5

Barak and Deborah were *in concert* in two senses. Their concerted military action — they worked together to save Israel — is described in Judges 4. The second sense is recorded in chapter 5 in the song that they sang together: 'On that day Deborah and Barak sang this song' (5:1). The two chapters must be understood together. The former records the historical events and the latter interprets them as the events are reflected on in the song. What we have here are really two views of the one concert. Among all the details, we should avoid being sidetracked by minor things. There are three main issues here.

1. The end of peace
2. The end of oppression
3. The end of Sisera

The end of peace

The good news is that 'the land had peace for eighty years' (3:30). However, when Ehud died 'the Israelites once again did evil in the eyes of the LORD' (4:1). This brought an end to the peace. The Lord gave them over to the oppression of Jabin, a Canaanite king. It was a terrible time: 'He had nine hundred iron chariots and had cruelly oppressed the Israelites for twenty years' (4:3).

It was not safe to travel and those who did used back roads: 'The roads were abandoned; travellers took to winding paths' (5:6). There was severe disruption to normal life under the military regime of Jabin and Sisera, the head of his army. Great trauma is implied by the summary observation that: 'Village life in Israel ceased' (5:7).

Idolatry was on the increase. Scripture was ignored and Israel became worldly and ecumenical: 'They chose new gods' (5:8). The venues for justice and settling disputes (the city gates) became places of hostility: 'War came to the city gates' (5:8). Sisera had so thoroughly disarmed Israel that armed warriors were non-existent: 'Not a shield or a spear was seen among forty thousand in Israel' (5:8).

But God was merciful. He pitied Israel and raised up Deborah as a judge and prophetess. She in turn summoned Barak from seven miles away in Kedesh, and when he came she revealed to him what God had commanded: 'She sent for Barak ... and said to him, "The LORD, the God of Israel, commands you: 'Go, take with you ten thousand men of Naphtali and Zebulun and lead the way to Mount Tabor. I will lure Sisera, the commander of Jabin's army, with his chariots and his troops to the Kishon River and give him into your hands"'" (4:6–7). It speaks highly of Barak's character and reputation that he was so readily able to get 10,000 men to go with him. They risked even worse oppression and disaster, outnumbered and outgunned by their cruel enemy. But at the command of God they went.

The Kishon River flowed down from Mt Tabor northwest into the Mediterranean Sea. Barak assembled his 10,000 men on top of Mt Tabor. Sisera was down on the plains below, his 900 iron chariots suited for the level ground of the broad Plain of Esdraelon in the valley of Megiddo. It was an intimidating scene facing Barak and his ill-equipped 10,000. As they looked down the valley they saw Sisera's professional hordes, soldiers armed with the latest military hardware. It was not an enviable task! Barak did not know how God would intervene. But he was a man of faith. The New Testament says that Barak was one 'who through faith conquered kingdoms, administered justice, and gained what was promised' (Heb. 11:33). He is a role model for us, a champion of the faith.

This raises the question of how we interpret his words to Deborah: 'Barak said to her, "If you go with me, I will go; but if you don't go with me, I won't go"' (4:8). There is a critical view that sees this as cowardice and weakness in Barak, as if he is hiding behind a woman. But this view is quite untenable. Everything we know about Barak indicates a robust and courageous warrior.

Regardless, how would the presence of one woman help his military chances? Was Deborah a warrior skilled in hand-to-hand combat?

The moralistic approach to this text ignores the context and tarnishes Deborah. Why did she willingly go along with Barak if his request was so unworthy and cowardly? Why did she not challenge his integrity? She was in the best position to understand Barak's words and motives, and her response was positive. She did accompany Barak but not to fight as a warrior. What was her role?

The truth is that Barak had a good and proper reason for seeking Deborah's company. Who was Deborah and what was her significance in Israel? The writer answers: 'Deborah, a prophetess, the wife of Lappidoth, was leading Israel at that time' (4:4). She was a prophetess. She was the agent of direct revelations from God. She was God's instrument for instructing and guiding Israel in those days. God told Israel his will by first revealing it to Deborah. It was her task to transmit the word of God to the people whenever prophetic disclosures occurred.

And this was exactly what she was doing in this context. She told Barak that the Lord wanted him to take 10,000 men to Mt Tabor where victory over Sisera would occur. Barak wanted Deborah to come with him to keep him posted on any other directions from God as they were revealed, directions about strategy in the battle. Because he knew the importance of God's word, Barak also recognized the importance of Deborah. His request was wise not cowardly. But we cannot avoid the conclusion that he said too much.

He went one step too far by making his own obedience conditional on Deborah's company. Deborah drew attention to his presumption. She prophesied that the honour of killing Sisera would not be for Barak but for a woman (Jael). "'Very well,' Deborah said, 'I will go with you. But because of the way you are going about this, the honour will not be yours, for the LORD will hand Sisera over to a woman'" (4:9). With or without Deborah, God had told Barak quite plainly to go to Mt Tabor. He had no right to add a condition to his obedience. This interpretation is consistent with the data.

THINK ABOUT IT

Women have a valuable role to play in the kingdom of God, both in and outside the church. Apart from honouring Christ with their gifts in many career paths, there are numerous ministries for Christian women to undertake in the church.[1] Perhaps this truth has been overshadowed in the modern debate about women's ordination, such that competent godly women are underused. This is lamentable and should be addressed, but ordination is not a biblical option.

The fact that there were prophetesses like Deborah in the Old Testament is not an argument for ordaining women today any more than the existence of male prophets implies that there are still prophets today. The book of Hebrews shows that Old Testament institutions belonged to the Jewish theocracy, the pre-Messianic age of shadows, whose substance was realized in Christ. There is no rational case for continuity of the former offices of judge, prophet, prophetess, priest, king or Levite in the church today.

The end of oppression

How could such a hastily formed band of recruits, with minimal weaponry, defeat Sisera's professional military outfit? What hope would Israel have on the plains around Megiddo and Taanach, five miles apart? The 900 enemy chariots would have a field day. Nevertheless, Barak took the battle down onto their home ground, where Sisera held all the advantages: 'So Barak went down Mount Tabor, followed by ten thousand men' (4:14). There he defeated Sisera's hordes, putting an end to oppression, but how?

As always, the battle belongs to the Lord. Behind all human events the hand of God works out his purposes, and it happened again that day. The text interprets the battle for us: '"This is the day the LORD has given Sisera into your hands. Has not the LORD gone ahead of you?" ... The LORD routed Sisera and all his chariots and army' (4:14–15).

The Lord normally uses secondary causes although he does not need them. He used Barak and his 10,000 men. But he also used another instrument: 'From the heavens the stars fought, from their courses they fought against Sisera. The river Kishon swept them away, the age-old river, the river Kishon' (5:20–21). In this poetic expression God's heavenly creatures represent him. To say that the stars fought against Sisera from the heavens means that God fought against Sisera. The Lord sent a flash flood, swelling the river Kishon into a torrent. It swept over its banks making the ground soft and muddy. Sisera's horses and chariots were now a hindrance. Their riders were frustrated and forced to abandon them in the bog. As they fled on foot Barak's men had the upper hand. They were travelling light and quickly overtook them.

There is a timeless principle here. Never underestimate the resources of the almighty God! If you have nothing else but God you are on the winning side. If you have everything else except God your case is hopeless. How easily God can turn certain defeat into victory! How easily the Almighty changes the strengths of an enemy into hindrances!

The question is, are you like Barak? Are you committed to the almighty God? If so then no matter how great your need, God is more than sufficient to meet your need. If God is for us, who is against us? His grace is sufficient for you to obey anything he requires you to do. How committed are you? This is a major theme in Judges 4 and 5.

Praise God for commitment! This is what the song is about. Deborah and Barak's concert rejoiced in the committed followers of God: 'On that day Deborah and Barak son of Abinoam sang this song: "When the princes in Israel take the lead, when the people willingly offer themselves — praise the LORD!'" (5:1–2). The song thanks God for those who work energetically in the service of his kingdom: 'My heart is with Israel's princes, with the willing volunteers among the people. Praise the LORD!' (5:9).

But where are the others? As in the church today, there were some uncommitted, half-hearted, inactive, nominal members in Israel. The song laments this fact. We are told that only six of the twelve tribes were represented in Barak's army: Zebulun, Naphtali, Ephraim, Benjamin, Issachar and Machir (the half tribe of Manasseh, named after his only son). Where were all the rest? The answer is given in 5:15–17.

Near the Dead Sea, the Reubenites stayed home to look after their farms (see map on page 105). They were among their campfires and flocks, but they had pangs of conscience: 'much searching of heart' (5:16). They felt their guilt.

The Gileadites were running true to form. Consisting of the tribe of Gad and the half tribe of Manasseh, they were always fringe dwellers in Israel, never even bothering to cross the Jordan into the promised land: 'Gilead stayed beyond the Jordan' (5:17).[2] There was no commitment there. Today, such people are associated with the church but only from a distance and only when it suits them.

For the Danites, business interfered with their commitment. They were too busy trading and making a shekel. The writer asks rhetorically, 'And Dan, why did he linger by the ships?' (5:17). Asher was too busy relaxing to fight for God's kingdom: 'Asher remained on the coast and stayed in his coves' (5:17). Asher enjoyed sheltered relaxing havens.

But those who went with Barak and Deborah are described as committed: 'The people of Zebulun risked their very lives; so did Naphtali on the heights of the field' (5:18). This is a universal gospel principle. Jesus Christ demands and deserves precisely this level of commitment. Anyone not willing to make a sacrifice is unworthy of being his disciple. Each of us needs to examine our level of commitment.

The end of Sisera

All the troops of Sisera fell by the sword; not a man was left. Sisera, however, fled on foot to the tent of Jael, the wife of Heber the Kenite, because there were friendly relations between Jabin king of Hazor and the clan of Heber the Kenite. Jael went out to meet Sisera and said to him, 'Come, my lord, come right in. Don't be afraid.' So he entered her tent, and she put a covering over him. 'I'm thirsty,' he said. 'Please give me some water.' She opened a skin of milk, gave him a drink, and covered him up. 'Stand in the doorway of the tent,' he told her. 'If someone comes by and asks you, "Is

Israel at the time of Deborah and Barak

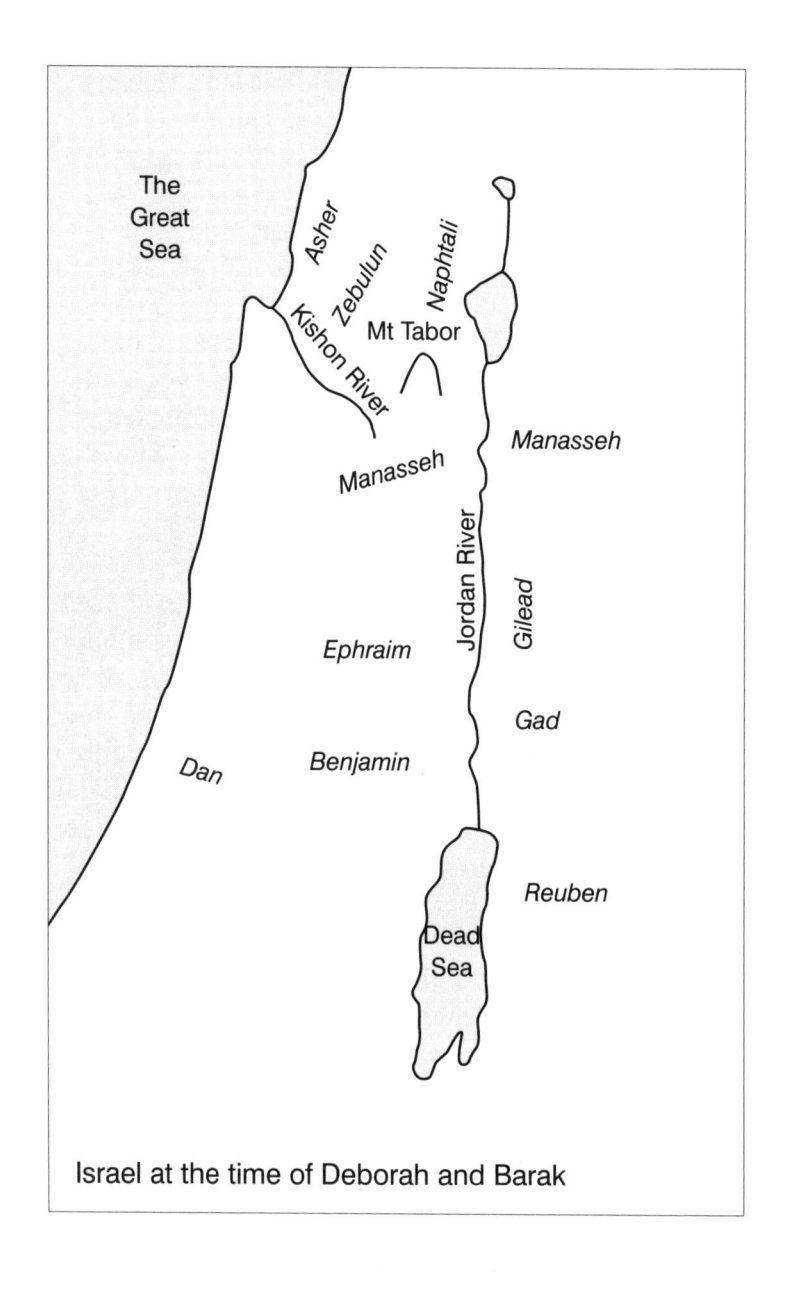

anyone here?" say "No."' But Jael, Heber's wife, picked up a tent peg and a hammer and went quietly to him while he lay fast asleep, exhausted. She drove the peg through his temple into the ground, and he died. Barak came by in pursuit of Sisera, and Jael went out to meet him. 'Come,' she said, 'I will show you the man you're looking for.' So he went in with her, and there lay Sisera with the tent peg through his temple — dead. On that day God subdued Jabin, the Canaanite king, before the Israelites (4:16–23).

How are we to evaluate the actions of Jael? Let us not rush in like humanists, denouncing her as a ghastly, treacherous woman. It is important to think biblically about her. How does the Bible regard Jael? What is the infallible and inspired interpretation of her disposing of Sisera? The answer features in the song of praise in chapter 5:

> Most blessed of women be Jael, the wife of Heber the Kenite, most blessed of tent-dwelling women. He asked for water, and she gave him milk; in a bowl fit for nobles she brought him curdled milk. Her hand reached for the tent peg, her right hand for the workman's hammer. She struck Sisera, she crushed his head, she shattered and

pierced his temple. At her feet he sank, he fell; there he lay. At her feet he sank, he fell; where he sank, there he fell — dead (5:24–27).

This is the judgement of Scripture: 'Most blessed of women be Jael.' Barak and Deborah rejoiced about Jael and her actions.

If Jael was evil then you must also criticize Barak and Deborah for calling her good. Indeed they are worse, for they made a song about it. They were ecstatically happy about Jael's actions! They even offered it as worship to God: 'I will sing to the LORD, I will sing; I will make music to the LORD, the God of Israel' (5:3). It was their prayer. They ended the song wishing that there had been more of it: 'So may all your enemies perish, O LORD! But may they who love you be like the sun when it rises in its strength' (5:31). You cannot attack Jael without attacking the Word of God. A low view of Jael is a low view of Scripture because Scripture has a high view of Jael.

It is important that we see the gospel paradigm here. It was an honour to kill God's wicked enemy, Sisera. Deborah had prophesied that the honour would not be given to Barak: 'The LORD will hand Sisera over to a woman' (4:9). So the integrity of prophecy is at stake. The integrity of God is involved. God is honouring Jael by allowing her to smite the enemy of Israel. Sisera was in solidarity with Satan, the serpent of old. Jael was in solidarity with the promised Saviour, the 'seed of the woman'. He came to 'crush the head' of the serpent.

THINK ABOUT IT

Jael crushing Sisera's head, David stoning Goliath's head (1 Sam. 17) and Christ crushing Satan's head all belong to the same gospel paradigm. It is part of the drama of salvation history. The imagery of 'head crushing' is not merely incidental. It belongs to the very nature of biblical revelation. God reveals his purposes by both word and event: 'Surely God will crush the heads of his enemies' (Ps. 68:21).

WHAT THE TEXT TEACHES

Those critical of Jael not only ignore this paradigm, but they make wrong assumptions. They commonly assume that Jael deliberately enticed Sisera inside by deceiving him with false security, feigning hospitality and betraying the long-standing peace between their two households. It is alleged that she deceived him by giving him milk when he only asked for water and a bed to sleep in. In summary, they assume it was premeditated murder. But the evidence does not demand that view.

There is an alternative explanation. It is possible that Jael initially received Sisera as she would have done in the past, genuinely and in good faith, with no harmful intentions at all. What ulterior motive could she have? Would she not be honoured to give hospitality to the region's leading warrior? If that possibility is conceded the subsequent events make good sense. The reconstructed scene may well be as follows.

While Sisera slept Jael began to realize that something was wrong. Why is Sisera here as an exhausted fugitive and not the victorious warrior that he has always been? Why is this man frightened enough to ask a woman to guard the door while he sleeps? Then Jael found out what had happened that day. The text does not say how, but it is clear that she knew that Barak was hunting for Sisera because when she saw him coming she went out to meet him. Then she said, 'Come ... I will show you the man you're looking for' (4:22). How did she know that? Perhaps other fugitives had told her as they ran by.

One thing is clear; she had heard the facts. She learned that *Yahweh* had fought Canaan and won. She knew that Barak's army had defeated Sisera's army. Like Rahab in Jericho, Jael must now make a decision. Who is my neighbour here and who is my enemy? This is not simply a matter of self-interest, it is a matter of spiritual alignment. It is a question of religion. It is gospel to the core. Would she now line up with the idols of Canaan or with *Yahweh* the God of Israel? She made the right choice. Death came quickly to Sisera, that cruel man whose oppression of the Hebrew people for twenty years made him notorious. This interpretation is fully consistent with biblical facts.

We leave this concert with its most solemn verse echoing in our ears: '"Curse Meroz," said the angel of the LORD. "Curse its people bitterly, because they did not come to help the LORD, to help the LORD against the mighty'" (5:23). Meroz was a town of Hebrew settlers who were merely Jews by name, religious nominals. They had no commitment to God at all, no zeal for the people of God, the truth of God or the cause of God. They were only in it for personal benefits.

This is not to be dismissed as a savage and sub-Christian sentiment. It is a universal truth found in the New Testament also: 'If anyone does not love the Lord — a curse be on him' (1 Cor. 16:22). Cursed is Meroz! Cursed are the uncommitted! 'He who is not with me is against me, and he who does not gather with me scatters' (Matt. 12:30).

QUESTIONS FOR DISCUSSION

1. What are the similarities between the song of Deborah and Barak (Judg. 5) and the songs of Moses and Miriam (Exod. 15:1–21)?

2. How does the principle of conduct commended by the following texts differ from fanaticism? (See Matt. 10:32–42; 16:24–25; Luke 10:25–28; 1 Cor. 10:31.)

3. How can legitimate cries for vengeance (like those in Acts 8:20; 1 Cor. 16:22; Gal. 1:8–9; 5:12; Rev. 6:10) be reconciled with Romans 12:19–21?

THE GUIDE

CHAPTER EIGHT

LEARNING FROM GIDEON (PART 1)

BIBLE READING

Judges 6:1–7:15

INTRODUCTION

Gideon admits to being a very ordinary person: "'But Lord,' Gideon asked, 'how can I save Israel? My clan is the weakest in Manasseh and I am the least in my family'" (6:15). He had no great ambitions and was virtually dragged into a key leadership role. Like all men he had feet of clay. One moment we see him acting commendably, and then he disappoints us. This is exactly why we can learn from Gideon. If God mightily used this ordinary man he can do the same with us.

Israel had forty years of peace following the victory of Deborah and Barak (6:1–10). After this, once again Israel acted wickedly. So the Lord sent Midianite hordes to oppress them for seven years. These desert nomads did not oppress Israel in the usual way. Rather than permanently occupying the territory, they would return each year in droves just before harvest time (6:3). They would seize the crops and cause untold damage: 'They ruined the crops all the way to Gaza and did not spare a living thing for Israel, neither sheep nor cattle nor donkeys' (6:4).

These mixed bands of 'Midianites, Amalekites and other eastern peoples' (6:3) were devastating like a plague of locusts: 'They came up with their livestock and their tents like swarms of locusts. It was impossible to count the men and their camels; they invaded the land to ravage it' (6:5). So terrible was the oppression that the Israelites left their homes and lived in 'mountain clefts, caves and strongholds' (6:2). They scraped whatever meagre existence they could from the land: 'Midian so impoverished the Israelites that they cried out to the LORD for help' (6:6). In his mercy God raised up a new judge to save them, Gideon, the son of Joash. He led Israel to victory in a most unusual battle against incredible odds.

His leadership has two distinct stages. In this chapter we will consider his preparation for battle (6:1–7:15), and in the next chapter we will consider the battle and its aftermath (7:15–8:35). The preparatory stage includes spiritual preparation, military preparation and emotional preparation.

Spiritual preparation

The narrative shows how God prepared Gideon in four ways: by preaching (6:7–10), by theophany (6:11–24), by reformation (6:25–32) and by condescension (6:36–40).

Preaching

Even before enlisting Gideon, God's first step in saving Israel was to send them a preacher, an unnamed prophet

(6:7–10). It was important preparation for all of Israel, including Gideon. The preacher's message was plain and pointed:

> This is what the LORD, the God of Israel, says: I brought you up out of Egypt, out of the land of slavery. I snatched you from the power of Egypt and from the hand of all your oppressors. I drove them from before you and gave you their land. I said to you, 'I am the LORD your God; do not worship the gods of the Amorites, in whose land you live.' But you have not listened to me (6:8).

The preacher first reminded them of the great works that God had lovingly done for Israel by delivering them from Egypt and giving them the vast promised land. Israel had so quickly forgotten her spiritual roots. Then he rebuked them for failing to obey God. Israel had adopted the ungodly ways of the pagans around them. The real enemy of Israel was Israel itself, not the Midianites!

There is a universal truth here. Whenever the church is in trouble and its enemies are getting the upper hand, the place to start looking is within. Look for unfaithfulness and departure from God's Word inside the church! Look for pulpits that no longer expound and apply the Word of God with integrity! Look for worldliness in the church!

God was about to revive Israel, and true revival begins with the type of preaching that this prophet gave. Such preaching is plain, applied, biblical and courageous enough to confront the real problems. Revival begins with preaching that honours the Word of God as authoritative, demanding radical repentance.

THINK ABOUT IT

Revival is painful and disruptive. Unbiblical ways of thinking and behaving creep into the church and corrupt it. Many of our unbiblical practices, traditions and opinions may have been in the church for a long time, but they have to go! May God give us more preachers like this unnamed man! The Word of God has to be central in everything we do. It has to stand supreme in everything — our songs, our prayers, our pulpits, our fellowship and our behaviour. If not, we are repeating the errors of Israel and asking for trouble.

Theophany

God reassured Gideon by sending the angel of the LORD (6:11–24). In our previous studies of this key figure we noted that the angel of the LORD is God himself appearing in temporary human form. To prepare Gideon for his work God appeared and said, 'I will be with you, and you will strike down all the Midianites together' (6:16). Then the divine visitor confirmed his words with miraculous signs, and Gideon was left with no doubts (6:16–21).

Reformation

To further strengthen and refine Gideon, God commanded him to take a strong stand against idolatry in Israel (6:25–32). He was to begin in his own father's house, using a young bull to pull down the altar of Baal and the Asherah pole beside it. It is helpful to know that archaeological diggings at Megiddo, not far from Ophrah, found an altar to Baal made of rocks cemented together measuring twenty-six square feet at the base and four and a half feet high. A bull would be needed to pull it down.

Gideon did his iconoclastic task by night because he was afraid (6:27). We should not be too critical. The context shows that his fears were well founded. He knew that it would cause outrage. Gideon is to be commended because he did not let his fear stop him from obeying God. He worked out a sensible way of dealing with his fear so that he could still obey. We should do the same.

The writer candidly shows the degree to which ordinary families had degenerated. Not only did Joash and his family worship idols, but they also had their own pagan shrine in the backyard! The same is true today, sin usually comes into the church after it has first settled into the homes and hearts of church members.

Sin hardens people. How did they respond when Gideon tore down the idols? Did they feel stricken in conscience and praise God for such good leadership? Did they sense a revival and reformation? No, they were baying for blood: 'The men of the town demanded of Joash, "Bring out your son. He must die, because he has broken down Baal's altar and cut down the Asherah pole beside it"' (6:30). You would think that a return to godliness might bring joy, especially with the sermon of the unnamed prophet still ringing in their ears. But as always, sin desensitizes people. It gets such a grip on us that we protect and institutionalize the sin, attacking people like Gideon who confront it. The more we indulge sin and the longer we accept it, the stronger its grip is on us. May God help us learn this truth from Gideon. Let us nip sin in the bud before it strangles us.

The fruits of reformation were immediate. Unexpectedly, Joash defended his son Gideon. 'Joash replied to the hostile crowd around him, "Are you going to plead Baal's cause? Are you trying to save him? Whoever fights for him shall be put to death by morning! If Baal really is a god, he can defend himself when someone breaks down his altar"' (6:31). His point was that if Baal is really a god he will not stand for someone desecrating his altar and mocking him as Gideon has done. Surely Baal can defend himself, and if he does not, he is not worth worrying about. This reasoning appealed to the bloodthirsty mob and they calmed down.

Condescension

> Gideon said to God, 'If you will save Israel by my hand as you have promised — look, I will place a

wool fleece on the threshing floor. If there is dew only on the fleece and all the ground is dry, then I will know that you will save Israel by my hand, as you said.' And that is what happened. Gideon rose early the next day; he squeezed the fleece and wrung out the dew — a bowlful of water. Then Gideon said to God, 'Do not be angry with me. Let me make just one more request. Allow me one more test with the fleece. This time make the fleece dry and the ground covered with dew.' That night God did so. Only the fleece was dry; all the ground was covered with dew (6:36–40).

WHAT THE TEXT TEACHES

This part of Gideon's spiritual preparation should never have occurred. If we let the clear principles of Scripture interpret this incident, we have to conclude that Gideon erred here. He was putting God to the test by asking for a miraculous sign.

God had already plainly given directions to Gideon. The Lord had appeared and spoken directly to Gideon: 'I will be with you, and you will strike down the Midianites together' (6:16). This plain word of God should have been enough. It needed no confirmation. However, God had already confirmed his word by a sign (16:17–22). Gideon knew that it was God talking to him.

Now Gideon is again asking God for a sign (God making only the fleece wet): 'then I will know that you will save Israel by my hand, as you said' (6:37). God graciously condescended to this request, but Gideon reneged, asking for yet another miracle — the previous one in reverse. He broke an assurance given to God.

Gideon was given direct guidance from the Lord. There was one single thing to do. For us, guidance comes from the Word of God, the Bible, alone. Scripture often leaves a wide number of options — where to work or live, who to marry or what career path to follow. There is a lot of freedom as long as we obey the revealed Word of God and act according to its general principles. We cannot go wrong if we stay consistent with Bible truths.

REMEMBER THIS

We are not to be 'putting out fleeces' like Gideon. It is true that God co-operated here, but God's gracious condescension to an erring child is not his stamp of approval. The Lord often blesses our mistakes because he is forbearing and patient, but this is not an argument for the mistake. God knows that we are feeble like dust, so he pities us as frail and erring children. There is no avoiding the fact that: 'A wicked and adulterous generation looks for a miraculous sign' (Matt. 16:4).

Military preparation

At first Gideon was outnumbered four to one. His army was a mere 32,000 against the 135,000 Midianites. But

God was determined to make the odds far worse so that no one could boast in the arm of flesh. Human strength is prone to deny God. We need to remember this! So the army was reduced in two stages.

First it went from 32,000 to 10,000. Gideon was instructed to say, 'Anyone who trembles with fear may turn back' (7:3). There was a provision in the Mosaic Law (Deut. 20:8) that allowed any timid soldiers to go home so that their fear would not undermine the morale of the others. Gideon would have expected some losses but not 22,000! This seventy per cent reduction must have shocked him. But God said that this was still too many.

The 10,000 were then reduced to 300 (a further ninety-seven per cent reduction). Those who knelt to drink were dismissed, but those who lapped water out of their hands were kept. This incident should not be moralized to mean that good soldiers lapped whereas careless ones knelt down. Are we to believe that out of the remaining brave warriors, those 10,000 fearless men in Israel, only 300 were suitable soldiers?

No. God reduced the army and increased the odds to 450:1 to prove that he is the cause of victory — not men. The drinking was purely arbitrary. There is nothing right or wrong in either method of drinking. He could have used other arbitrary methods to distinguish the men, such as those who slept flat on the ground and those who had a pillow under their head. Because God was ensuring that all of the glory would go to him, it is far easier to argue that the best soldiers were sent away and the remaining 300 were the unskilled and inexperienced. However, this is not a moral issue.

There is a valid application here for us today. God not only desires to give his people victory but to teach us humility. If our victories and achievements make us more self-reliant, they are more disastrous than defeat. You cannot be too small or too insignificant for God to use, but you can be too big! 'God chose the weak things of the world to shame the strong. He chose the lowly things of this world and the despised things — and the things that are not — to nullify the things that are, so that no one may boast before him' (1 Cor. 1:27–29).

The church is on the wrong track when it thinks in terms of needing more troops, more 'horsepower' or more great and gifted ones before it can bear a fruitful harvest. No, we need the Lord God, and if we are obedient to him nothing can stand before us. We need humble, faithful and obedient people, and even if we are outnumbered 450:1 we will do things beyond all expectations: 'Now to him who is able to do immeasurably more than all we ask or imagine, according to his power that is at work within us' (Eph. 3:20).

Emotional preparation

Gideon was now spiritually ready and militarily prepared, but he was emotionally unsettled. He was still

WHAT THE TEXT TEACHES

fearful of attacking the enemy hordes, so the Lord graciously prepared him through something dreamed by a Midianite. God told Gideon: 'If you are afraid to attack, go down to the camp with your servant Purah and listen to what they are saying. Afterward, you will be encouraged to attack the camp' (7:10–11). And it was so.

Gideon arrived just as a man was telling a friend his dream: 'I had a dream,' he was saying. 'A round loaf of barley bread came tumbling into the Midianite camp. It struck the tent with such force that the tent overturned and collapsed.' His friend responded, 'This can be nothing other than the sword of Gideon son of Joash, the Israelite. God has given the Midianites and the whole camp into his hands.' When Gideon heard the dream and its interpretation, he worshipped God. He returned to the camp of Israel and called out, 'Get up! The LORD has given the Midianite camp into your hands' (7:13–15).

God's kindness is prominent here. What remarkable measures he is prepared to take for the comfort of his people! In his sovereign arrangements the Lord ensured that the Midianite had the dream, directed Gideon's feet to that man's tent, timing it perfectly for him to hear the dream related and interpreted, and protected Gideon from being discovered.

God is concerned for our emotional well-being and provides the means of grace to comfort us. These will not be the unusual means that Gideon was given because his situation was extraordinary. We use the usual means of grace. We have far more to encourage us than Gideon. We have the finished work of Christ, the complete Bible and the Holy Spirit more richly outpoured. God cared for Gideon, a most ordinary man, so take heart! God did great things through Gideon against great odds. Compared with God's people even conquerors are losers! 'We are more than conquerors through him who loved us' (Rom. 8:37).

QUESTIONS FOR DISCUSSION

1. *What principles for spiritual revival can be fairly deduced from the following texts? (2 Chr. 7:14; Isa. 59:1–3; Jer. 5:24–31; 6:10–15; Hosea 14:1–9; Rev. 2:12–17.)*

2. *What characteristics of good preaching can be deduced from the following texts? (Neh. 8:1–3; John 5:39–40; Acts 20:17–21; 1 Tim. 4; Titus 1:7–2:15; James 3:1.)*

… THE GUIDE

CHAPTER NINE

LEARNING FROM GIDEON (PART 2)

BIBLE READING

Judges 7:16–8:35

As we consider Gideon in action we can learn from his victory, his wisdom and his folly.

His victory

Gideon's victory against odds of 450:1 is quite famous. It ranks with David and Goliath as a favourite Bible story. But how well is it understood? How much practical learning has the Christian church derived from shrewd thinking that maximized the effects of a small team?

A well-prepared Gideon was now ready to act. He was at the point of thorough conviction and confidence when he told his army: 'Get up! The LORD has given the Midianite camp into your hands' (7:15). But what did this confident Gideon do? Did he appear on the battlefield randomly, without a strategic plan? Did he presume that God would do his thinking for him? Was Gideon strong on divine sovereignty but weak on human responsibility? No! He had a clever strategy with several noteworthy features.

He divided his troops into three companies. When they went down the hillsides into the valley where the Midianites were camped, the approach from three sides made Midian feel surrounded.

Gideon was a pioneer of 'surround-sound' technology. His plan used instruments designed to maximize impact. The smashing of clay pots would echo around the hills in the still of night. The torches suddenly appearing on three sides would look like a rush of warriors, striking fear into every heart. The shrill blasts from many trumpets would give the inflated impression of a massive army. Even in a large army there are normally only a few trumpeters.

Also, Gideon found their weak spot and exploited it. He struck at the most advantageous time of 10:00 p.m.: '...the beginning of the middle watch' (7:19). The enemy was more vulnerable then because the sentries were being changed. Those going on duty would be wiping sleep from their eyes and not ready for battle. Those going off duty would still be walking about the camp and might well appear as enemies to anyone suddenly wakened from sleep by the sound of trumpets.

The combined effect of the confusion plus the repeated lusty war cry: 'A sword for the LORD and for Gideon!'(7:20), hurled the camp into such disarray that 'all the Midianites ran, crying out as they fled' (7:21). It is not uncommon for people suddenly wakened from sleep to be in a state of panic, not thinking straight. They imagined that the enemy was right on them and that everyone they saw was one of Gideon's men. In desperate panic they thrust their swords this way and that causing significant collateral damage, killing off their own troops. What lessons can we properly derive from this?

We learn that faith is intelligent. Trusting God does not preclude the need for a clear and intelligent plan of action. There are some Christians who think that it is unspiritual to pour intellectual effort into planning aims, goals and strategies for the church. There is a very dangerous and suave sounding piety that shuns good planning, as if it was an attempt to manipulate God. The assumption is that God will simply bypass our minds and efforts, somehow mystically leading us into what we should say and do. Psalm 46:10 is often misquoted in this way: 'Be still, and know that I am God.' Vague mantras roll piously off the tongue: 'be open to the leading of the Holy Spirit' or 'let go and let God'. But these sayings fail under scrutiny.

If Gideon had followed this mystical advice he would have trooped down to Midian with nothing particular in mind. He would have stood unarmed before the enemy saying prayerfully: 'Here we are Lord, ready and waiting — use us as you will!' It may sound very pious but it is actually tempting God. It is foolish, presumptuous and an insult to God and a denial of the brainpower and reasoning faculty that our Maker has given us. We cannot expect fruitfulness in the kingdom of God if, as individuals or churches, we merely exist waiting for whatever happens. Vagueness and victory do not match! We need to take initiatives, set goals, make plans and pursue them, trusting God to honour his promise: 'And surely I am with you always, to the very end of the age' (Matt. 28:20).

There is no single *right plan* fitting all Christians at all points in history. Our strategy has to fit the culture and circumstances before us. Gideon's method was not the same as that of Barak, Samson or Shamgar. Gideon's method was most unusual, uniquely suited for Gideon's exact circumstances. He got the maximum advantage from small numbers walking down the hillsides at night. But this plan would have been foolish if he had been in Barak's situation. What good are clay pots and torches on the vast plains of Megiddo in broad daylight? How would that frighten Sisera's army and his iron chariots? They would have slaughtered Israel.

As we work to promote the gospel in our neighbourhood it is no good harking back to some method that worked well in the past. We must engage people in their current situation. A lot has happened in thirty years. Biblical principles no longer permeate cultures where they once did. Australia, for example, is now very secular. Post-modern thinking affects even those who have never heard of it. We cannot assume that people have a Bible or know anything about it. Concepts familiar inside the church will not communicate outside, or they may communicate wrong ideas.

THINK ABOUT IT

With the deluge of inane and mundane things on countless televisions, the dumbing down of language gathers momentum. We live in a culture where ice cream is 'heavenly', we have 'faith' in our sporting heroes, a novel idea is a 'revelation' and 'Jesus' is merely one of the many common expletives. Therefore, we have to ask what the average person understands by terms like *salvation, sin, eternal life, hell* or *repentance*. We must use sanctified common sense in our interaction with men and women. They desperately need Christ communicated to them in unambiguous terms.

His wisdom

Three incidents in Judges 8 testify to Gideon's wisdom: the jealousy of Ephraim, the cowardice of Succoth and Peniel and the popularity of Gideon, who was under pressure to be made king.

The jealousy of Ephraim

'Now the Ephraimites asked Gideon, "Why have you treated us like this? Why didn't you call us when you went to fight Midian?" And they criticized him sharply' (8:1). Their complaint was that Gideon did not use them in the initial work, only calling on them after the first success (7:24–25). They were complaining needlessly and ignorantly. As readers we are privy to the reason why Gideon did not include Ephraim at the start of the battle. He was following God's strict orders. God only wanted a tiny group of 300 to do the job.

In his wisdom Gideon did not reply sharply to them. He could see that, for all of its faults, Ephraim was not like Succoth and Peniel. Ephraim at least did pitch in and help when asked, and they did it very well, capturing the two Midianite leaders (Oreb and Zeeb). So Gideon disarmed their contentious spirit by commending what they had done: 'God gave Oreb and Zeeb, the Midianite leaders, into your hands. What was I able to do compared to you? At this, their resentment against him subsided' (8:3). Gideon was saying that they captured the leaders, whereas he only got them on the run! Therefore, their success was greater than his. Consequently, Gideon's wisdom here shows how 'a gentle answer turns away wrath' (Prov. 15:1).

THINK ABOUT IT

Although integrity demands that some criticisms must be confronted it is not always the case. If personal attacks against us do not hinder the work of the Lord, why burn up energy countering them? Why not follow Gideon's lead? If it can be done without hypocrisy, let us encourage and praise our critics for their good work. Let a gentle answer defuse wrath. Such wisdom shuts down potentially vicious situations.

WHAT THE TEXT TEACHES

The cowardice of Succoth and Peniel

'Gideon and his three hundred men, exhausted yet keeping up the pursuit, came to the Jordan and crossed it. He said to the men of Succoth, "Give my troops some bread; they are worn out, and I am still pursuing Zebah and Zalmunna, the kings of Midian"' (8:4–5). But, because they refused, 'Gideon replied, "Just for that, when the LORD has given Zebah and Zalmunna into my hand, I will tear your flesh with desert thorns and briers"' (8:7).

The same scenario was repeated at Peniel. 'From there he went up to Peniel and made the same request of them, but they answered as the men of Succoth had. So he said to the men of Peniel, "When I return in triumph, I will tear down this tower"' (8:8–9). These cases required different solutions. Wisdom demanded leniency towards Ephraim but discipline for Succoth and Peniel because these two towns refused to commit themselves to the work of the Lord.

They wanted to have it both ways. They wanted Gideon to do the hard work of delivering them from Midian, but they also wanted to keep their options open in case Gideon failed. They did not want to be openly against the two kings of Midian (Zeba and Zalmunna) in case they won. If that happened they could cash in on their cowardice by pleading with them for leniency because they refused to help Gideon.

So both towns refused to help Gideon: 'Do you already have the hands of Zeba and Zalmunna in your possession? Why should we give bread to your troops?' (8:6). It amounted to unbelief, disloyalty and outright cowardice. It is a serious sin when people leave their options open between Christ and Satan (especially people in the church).

When Gideon returned as judge and civil magistrate in Israel, he extracted the strict justice and vengeance such ungodliness deserved. In Peniel he tore down a tower that was obviously important to them in some way, and he killed the men of the town. In Succoth, he interrogated a youth who told him the names of the seventy-seven town leaders. They were the ones who should have willingly supported Gideon. Gideon did exactly as he said: 'He took the elders of the town and taught the men of Succoth a lesson by punishing them with desert thorns and briers' (8:16).

Perhaps they were singled out because they hindered otherwise willing helpers. Presumably there were mitigating circumstances to explain why Gideon did not kill them as he had in Peniel. But he painfully and thoroughly disciplined them. Their flesh would have been ripped and torn apart. They would have been in agony for weeks, bearing lifelong scars as testimonies of their cowardice.

It takes wisdom for leaders in the church to distinguish between the childish complaints of otherwise loyal and committed people (like Ephraim) and the serious sins of uncommitted people (like Succoth). In the one case, mercy and gentle encouragement is in order. In the other case, strict church discipline is needed. When discipline is due (and the New Testament plainly indicates the sorts of issues where it is due) it must not be withheld. Of course the methods are not the same now, but the principle is.

The popularity of Gideon

'The Israelites said to Gideon, "Rule over us — you, your son and your grandson — because you have saved us out of the hand of Midian"' (8:22). But Gideon refused in the most unambiguous terms: 'I will not rule over you, nor will my son rule over you. The LORD will rule over you' (8:23). There is nothing wrong with Israel having a human king. It was God's purpose to give them a king, and the repeated theme of this book is the need for a king: 'In those days Israel had no king; everyone did as he saw fit' (17:6; 21:25). But the sort of king that Israel wanted was essentially pagan, in the manner of the surrounding nations.

They wanted a king *instead of* God, but the divine plan was a king *under* God, ruling like God and for God. Until they accepted the rule of God himself they were not ready for the rule of God via his anointed king. Ultimately Jesus Christ is that king, and the Old Testament monarchy was a shadowy paradigm that typified the rule of the coming messianic King. A few good kings were helpful, but the rest practically rejected the rule of God, doing Israel much harm. Thank God for men like Gideon whose esteem for the glory of God exceeded all personal ambitions, honours and rewards that men might confer on them.

His folly

And he said, 'I do have one request, that each of you give me an earring from your share of the plunder.' (It was the custom of the Ishmaelites to wear gold earrings.) They answered, 'We'll be glad to give them.' So they spread out a garment, and each man threw a ring from his plunder onto it. The weight of the gold rings he asked for came to seventeen hundred shekels, not counting the ornaments, the pendants and the purple garments worn by the kings of Midian or the chains that were on their camels' necks. Gideon made the gold into an ephod, which he placed in Ophrah, his town. All Israel prostituted themselves by worshipping it there, and it became a snare to Gideon and his family (8:24–27).

An ephod was a piece of richly ornamented clothing worn by the high priest, an apron covering both back and front. Why did Gideon make one? We can safely assume that he had good intentions. The last thing that he would have wanted was a return to the idolatry that he had just saved them from. It is also difficult to avoid the conclusion that the high priest at Shiloh was corrupt at that time. At no point in the book of Judges do we read of the high priest functioning as God intended. Even the high priesthood of a decent man like Eli was concurrent with serious immorality and abuses at the shrine (1 Sam. 2). Shiloh was given over to the idolatry of Baal worship. Understood in this context Gideon was attempting to reform Israel back to the worship of Jehovah. This good motive is especially likely because the incident follows after his refusal to be king. However, it was a foolish act.

The people did what Gideon never intended and worshipped the ephod itself. It was so rich and valuable that they revered it. The 1,700 shekels of gold adorning it equates to over two million dollars at today's value. It became a snare to Gideon and his family. It is a sick society that bows down to metal, cloth, wood and stone! But nothing has changed. It still goes on all over the world. We still venerate mere creatures, genuflecting and bowing down before them. It is still rank idolatry.

There are several lessons to be learned here. First, the church must only be reformed along biblical lines. Good motives are not enough. When the people of God go wrong, as Israel had, they have always departed from Scripture. Therefore, the way back (reformation) always has to be a return to what God says in his Word. Human leaders, including Gideon, have no right to reform the church according to their own ideas.

Another lesson is that even good men have hearts of iron and feet of clay! We must not think that everything done by reformers in the church is good. The actions of the very best leaders (like Gideon, Martin Luther or John Calvin) must be checked against Scripture. We must have a higher authority than men. Our only supreme standard is Scripture itself, and no man is exempt from its scrutiny. Refrain from blind loyalty to a Gideon or Calvin or any other leader.

It is instructive that God uses imperfect servants. When we read of the mistakes of believers like Gideon, be careful not to take the high moral ground. We should be grateful that the details of our lives are not recorded in the Bible for the whole human race to read. If God devoted two chapters to your life, would you come out as clean as Gideon, Noah, Moses or David?

Gideon was an ordinary man like us, he was not perfect, but God used him mightily. This gives us hope. We also have weaknesses and inconsistencies, and although God does not excuse or approve of them, he does not refuse to use us if we are not perfect. So let us press on and, like Gideon, do all that we can to serve the Lord. But let us learn to test all things against Scripture. Gideon did not have a full Bible. We do! To whom much is given shall much be required (see Luke 12:48).

QUESTIONS FOR DISCUSSION

1. Regarding plans for 'tomorrow' what precisely is being taught in James 3:13–16 and Matthew 6:24–34?

2. What are the implications of 1 Corinthians 14:8–11, 20–25 for churches today?

3. What factors determine whether a sin should be overlooked in love (Prov. 10:12; 1 Peter 4:8) or confronted by the formal processes of church discipline (Matt. 18:14–17)?

4. Why is discernment so important? (See Matt. 7:15–27; Eph. 4:11–18; Phil. 1:9–11; Jude 3–4; Rev. 13:14.)

THE GUIDE

CHAPTER TEN

A THORNY PROBLEM

LOOK IT UP

BIBLE READING

Judges 9

INTRODUCTION

To hear someone described as 'a thorn in the side' implies that they cause pain. Judges 9 introduces a man of multiple thorns. Prophetically called a 'thorn bush', his name is Abimelech, the illegitimate son of Gideon. He was a major hindrance to Israel and a source of many thorns in her side. A blight and curse on Israel, Abimelech caused civil war and violent bloodshed at an atrocious level. He was a thorny problem, just as Jotham described him in his parable of the trees and the thorn bush (9:8–15): 'Finally all the trees said to the thorn bush, "Come and be our king"' (9:14).

Abimelech was not a judge. He did not deliver Israel. On the contrary he oppressed it. This worthless fellow was crowned king in Shechem where he ruled for three years. He died when a woman dropped an upper millstone on him. Used to crush grain into flour, it was a stone wheel about two feet in diameter and about three inches thick, weighing about eighty pounds. Why then is this chapter in the book of Judges? It shows us that Israel's real enemy was not Moab, Philistia, Amon or the Canaanites. *Israel was its own worst enemy.*

Following Gideon were the two judges Tola and Jair. Between them they saved and led Israel for forty-five years (10:1–3). We are not told whether they delivered Israel from foreign powers, and there is no need to assume that they did. It is quite likely that they delivered Israel from its own internal problems and from the mess caused by men like Abimelech. For nearly half a century these judges dealt with the tribal wars, political intrigue and treachery caused by selfish brothers trampling over the interests of other brothers.

To grasp this portion of Scripture we need to understand two things regarding 'the thorny problem' it describes. We need to get the picture (understand the events) so that we can then get the point (learn the lessons).

Get the picture

The story begins with an election campaign. Abimelech means 'My father is king'. Ironically his father was not the king. Gideon had strenuously refused attempts to make him king (8:23). Abimelech could see that someone from Gideon's family was going to rule, possibly all seventy sons together, so he made his grab for power. He told the leaders in Shechem that he was their best choice. He ran his own 'vote for me' campaign: 'Ask all the citizens of Shechem, "Which is better for you: to have all seventy of Jerub-Baal's sons rule over you, or

WHAT THE TEXT TEACHES

just one man?" Remember, I am your flesh and blood' (9:2).

Abimelech was a ruthless politician. He gained the support of his seventy brothers and the people of Shechem. But as soon as he had cashed in on their votes they became expendable. In a callous plot to shore up his political security he murdered all of his potential opponents (his own brothers). He publicly executed his own family at one time and at one place: 'on one stone' (9:5).

How was this wicked man financed? It was by the corrupt Israel: 'They gave him seventy shekels of silver from the temple of Baal-Berith, and Abimelech used it to hire reckless adventurers, who became his followers' (9:4). Shechem's religious people backed this wretch and paid his stipend! They took a collection and he used it to pay his pack of 'worthless and reckless fellows' (NASV).

This was not the first or last time that an organized worldly corrupt 'church' supported wickedness. The *World Council of Churches* is a modern example. Sympathetic to the cries of 'liberation theology' it has given considerable sums of money to support revolutionary groups. In Brisbane we have witnessed the *Joint Church Social Justice Commission* giving full support to homosexuals. Each is a case of the same unholy principle: 'seventy shekels of silver from the temple of Baal-Berith' (9:4).

But God was already working to cause Abimelech's downfall. Jotham, the youngest of the seventy brothers, escaped: 'He [Jotham] climbed up on the top of Mount Gerizim and shouted to them, "Listen to me, citizens of Shechem, so that God may listen to you. One day the trees went out to anoint a king for themselves. They said to the olive tree, 'Be our king!'"' (9:7–8). In this parable of protest, the men who would have made worthy kings were symbolically designated as the olive tree, the fig tree and the vine. But they all declined.

So the trees asked the worthless thorn bush to rule over them. His acceptance was typically ominous: 'The thorn bush said to the trees, "If you really want to anoint me king over you, come and take refuge in my shade; but if not, then let fire come out of the thorn bush and consume the cedars of Lebanon!"' (9:15). In other words, unless you anoint me as king you will be sorry! Fire will come out from me and destroy you. The reality of course is that a thorn bush is good for nothing. A low wiry bush with few leaves, it offered no real shade or comfort, only pain. It aptly depicted Abimelech who had nothing worthwhile to offer Israel.

Then Jotham interpreted his parable: 'If then you have acted honourably and in good faith toward Jerub-Baal and his family today, may Abimelech be your joy, and may you be his, too! But if you have not, let fire come out from Abimelech and consume you ... and let fire come out from you ... and consume Abimelech!' (9:19–20). May you both get what you deserve from each other!

The rest of the narrative describes how God brought these words of Jotham to pass. In the first step God made use of an evil spirit:

> God sent an evil spirit between Abimelech and the citizens of Shechem, who acted treacherously against Abimelech. God did this in order that the crime against Jerub-Baal's seventy sons, the shedding of their blood, might be avenged on their brother Abimelech and on the citizens of Shechem, who had helped him murder his brothers (9:23–24).

How treacherous the support of wicked men really is! Abilemech's former supporters were now his enemies, lying in wait to ambush him (9:25). They teamed up with Gaal, a mercenary with his own band of reckless men. After a drunken party in their religious shrine, they plotted to kill Abimelech. But Zebul (the ruler of Shechem) still had some blind loyalty to Abimelech and so he warned him. Then he arranged for Gaal to go and fight Abimelech whom he knew was ready and waiting to spring an ambush. So Abimelech got rid of Gaal. But he was so angry that he destroyed the city of Shechem and sowed it with salt, indicating present defeat and future barrenness.

The leaders barricaded themselves inside the safest place, the innermost room of their cultic buildings, the temple of El-Berith. But Abimelech saw this as his window of opportunity, and he burned them alive. Still raging, Abimelech marched to another city, Thebez, capturing it too. He was about to burn down its tower also, to kill the many people hiding inside, when a woman dropped an upper millstone on him, crushing his head. Not wanting to die with the humiliation of being killed by a woman, he had his servant run him through with his sword. So Abimelech died.

But God will not be mocked. The writer ends this story by showing us that God had been at work in repaying Abimelech and his supporters: 'Thus God repaid the wickedness that Abimelech had done to his father by murdering his seventy brothers. God also made the men of Shechem pay for all their wickedness. The curse of Jotham son of Jerub-Baal came on them' (9:56–57).

Get the point

It is edifying to draw out the great ethical principles taught throughout the Bible, which are brought into sharp focus by the events of Judges 9. To begin with, we learn that God turns evil on itself. God is in complete control of evil and evil spirits (9:23–24). He uses them to bring about his own good purposes: 'The LORD works out everything for his own ends — even the wicked for a day of disaster' (Prov. 16:4). By putting an evil spirit between Abimelech and his supporters God made them self-destruct! They both got what they deserved. Divine justice prevailed and they were repaid for the violence done to the seventy sons of Gideon.

We must never forget that God can and does fight fire with fire. He will sometimes make Satan rip himself apart. Although God is not the author of evil, nor does he condone, promote or in any way support evil, neither is he an idle helpless bystander. God is not a victim. As the ruler of the universe he commands evil spirits to drown pigs, an evil spirit to torment proud Saul and an evil spirit to ruin the relationship between Abimelech and his supporters.

In doing this, God makes evil do what it hates most, namely to bring justice, truth and equity to bear. Like a good physician he knows how to milk the serpent and use his poison as antivenin. God causes Satan to fight Satan so that the evil house is divided against itself, and it cannot stand.

What an awesome God! In evil days we must learn not to be immobilized by pessimism. We cannot tell how and when the Almighty will use one form of evil to overcome another. Our God is in complete control, using both good and evil to accomplish amazing and unexpected results. Who would have known that the evil spirit would get rid of two evils in one, Abimelech and the Shechemites? We need texts like Judges 9 to make us say with Paul, 'Oh, the depth of the riches of the wisdom and knowledge of God! How unsearchable his judgements, and his paths beyond tracing out! "Who has known the mind of the Lord? Or who has been his counselor?"' (Rom. 11:33–34).

> ### REMEMBER THIS
>
> Take heart! The devil is not in control and never will be. Calvary is the supreme example of God using evil to overcome evil. Evil men did their worst, but they only finished up serving the cause they hated — the cause of truth, justice and divine vengeance. Wicked men crucified the Son of God in their blind hatred for the church, but in so doing they ensured the eternal life of the church, the salvation of sinners and the defeat of Satan! We must never presume to know how God is operating his secret will today.

This text also displays the nature of a true protestant. There is a combination of courage and wisdom in Jotham. He was courageous in resisting evil. He had a moral, a godly, a social and an outraged conscience. Like Martin Luther who centuries later nailed his theses to the Wittenberg church door, he stood on Mt Gerizim and loudly protested against evil toward God and in the society. He did not succumb to the many arguments that might have tempted him to be silent. He did not capitulate to pessimism.

This courageous man of God had high principles. He rebuked the evildoers and spoke out against evils against God and the state, crying out for God to vindicate him with holy vengeance. Jotham was brave but not foolhardy. He spoke from Mt Gerizim, a place where escape would be quick and easy. He took only necessary risks. We must learn to copy his example. On the one hand our personal safety is not to stop us from being faithful to God. If necessary, we are to forfeit our own lives in declaring the mind of God. On the other hand no amount of faithfulness warrants reckless disregard for safety. The early Christian martyrs illustrated the same truth. While free they resisted capture and preserved their lives 'on the run' and in hiding while they could. However, once captured they put honour for Christ above their own safety.

Another practical lesson is that sin breeds more sin. Sin always has serious consequences. Shakespeare was right: 'The evil that men do lives after them; the good is oft interred with their bones' (*Julius Caesar*, Act III, Scene 2). It was so with Gideon. The people soon forgot all the good that he had done for Israel. It was buried with his bones. But his sins caused great problems. He sinned by marrying many wives. By producing seventy sons he created the nursery from which dynastic struggles began. As we saw in chapter 8, Gideon had to shoulder the blame for reforming Israel along unbiblical lines because he made the golden ephod that became an idolatrous snare (8:27). Although he did not intend it, he facilitated the false religion that financed terror.

Moreover, Gideon had a mistress, a concubine. This led to a son being born out of marriage, the illegitimate Abimelech, a curse on his generation. Sin is never a private matter: it always has consequences for other people. What might appear as a private sin (jealousy, envy, bitterness, lust, covetousness or discontent) is not so private after all.

It is also important to notice the warped and twisted sense of values in godless men. They have wrong notions of what is important. When the woman dropped the millstone on his skull, Abimelech told his servant, 'Draw your sword and kill me, so that they can't say, "A woman killed him"' (9:54). Men are meticulous about trivia while they neglect the weighty matters of hell and judgement. Here is Abimelech just moments before plunging into eternal misery — yet all he can think about is 'dying like a man'! This was the only thing on his mind, the sum total of his system of values.

Millions of foolish people around us are just like Abimelech. Their values are warped. They care nothing for the precious blood of Christ or for the fact that they are spiritually lost. They have no idea of the reality of that great climactic moment of history when Christ returns and every eye will see him, every knee will bow, the books will be opened and every one will give an account to the Judge!

However, they are fastidious about all sorts of trivial things. They would hate to be thought of as a sloppy dresser, an unreliable member of their club, an untidy gardener or a poor housekeeper. So they are very careful to be well dressed and punctual. They take care of spotless homes with manicured gardens and washed and polished cars. Nobody can fault them on these matters, but all the time their hearts are vile and cold towards God. They are spiritually stained and unacceptable to God.

THINK ABOUT IT

Hell is full of people who were not killed by a woman! Hell is full of people who were excellent gardeners, good committee members and neat housekeepers who dressed well. Hell is full of punctual people who played a good bowling game. In the context of eternity, utter trivia clutters the minds of men! Why rearrange the deck chairs on the *Titanic*?

Infinite wisdom urges us to 'seek first the kingdom of God' (Matt. 6:33, NKJV). If we get this priority right everything else will fall into line.

QUESTIONS FOR DISCUSSION

1. *Abimelech is the proverbial 'fool'! Do you agree with this assessment? (See Prov. 10:14,23; 11:29; 12:16; 13:16; 14:16; 17:21; 20:3; 26:1; 29:11.)*

2. *What makes God's justice so serious? (See Lev. 24:15–23; Deut. 19:16–21; Prov. 17:3; 21:2; Jer. 17:10; 20:12; 2 Cor. 5:10; Rev. 20:11–13.)*

3. *'To deny that God uses evil spirits to accomplish his will is to deny the gospel!' Is this statement true? Read Revelation 12 and 20.*

THE GUIDE

CHAPTER ELEVEN

HAS JEPHTHAH BEEN DEFAMED?

BIBLE READING

Judges 10–12

INTRODUCTION

Jephthah has received very bad press. He was instrumental in saving Israel from eighteen years of Ammonite oppression, but it is traditional for Christians to accuse him of making a rash vow: 'And Jephthah made a vow to the LORD: "If you give the Ammonites into my hands, whatever comes out of the door of my house to meet me when I return in triumph ... will be the LORD's, and I will sacrifice it as a burnt offering'" (11:30–31). In the traditional view, Jephthah was a fool, promising to sacrifice the first living thing he saw coming out of his front door.

After returning home victorious, he was joyfully greeted by his daughter, his only child. His misery was instantaneous as the impact of his vow hit home. His daughter agreed that he must keep his word: "'My father," she replied, "you have given your word to the LORD. Do to me just as you promised'" (11:36). So Jephthah kept his vow. Did he kill his daughter? Was he guilty of making a human sacrifice, or has he been defamed? This is the issue we need to consider.

Consider the scene

It was about 1300 B.C., and the writer tells us candidly how dreadful the situation was.

> Again the Israelites did evil in the eyes of the LORD. They served the Baals and the Ashtoreths, and the gods of Aram, the gods of Sidon, the gods of Moab, the gods of the Ammonites and the gods of the Philistines. And because the Israelites forsook the LORD and no longer served him, he became angry with them. He sold them into the hands of the Philistines and the Ammonites, who that year shattered and crushed them. For eighteen years they oppressed all the Israelites on the east side of the Jordan in Gilead, the land of the Amorites (10:6–8).

They had the temerity to cry out for Jehovah to save them, but he said: 'You have forsaken me and served other gods, so I will no longer save you. Go and cry out to the gods you have chosen. Let them save you when you are in trouble!' (10:13–14). So they changed their ways and the LORD pitied them because 'he could bear Israel's misery no longer' (10:16).

THINK ABOUT IT

God is not a stone. To deny passions or emotions in God is a misuse of the doctrine of divine impassibility. God feels pity because he feels the misery of his people and he can

THINK ABOUT IT

no longer bear it. There is a real correspondence between human feelings and divine feelings: 'In all their distress he too was distressed' (Isa. 63:9). The Bible shows that God experiences anger, jealousy, joy, abhorrence and grief. Although some descriptions of divine activity are purely anthropomorphic, where there is no real analogy with the human experience (e.g., the finger of God, the arm of God, God changing his mind), other cases are far more complex (e.g., joy and grief).

Denying these emotions in God implies that he looks on both good and evil with the same stone-faced equanimity. Although he would perfectly distinguish them, he would feel the same about them. Rightly understood, divine impassibility denies passions in God that are in any way dysfunctional, passive or irrational. God is never a victim of breakdown, mental conflict or neurosis. Human suffering is often passive — something we could not anticipate or have any control over. But God is always in control. This issue becomes acute at Calvary. Did the Father crush his Son dispassionately? Did he turn his back on Christ effortlessly? Did he curse him with indifference? Is there nothing in the Father corresponding to that pang of dereliction in his Son: 'My God, My God, why have you forsaken me?' (Matt. 27:46). These are serious issues.[1]

In this context of divine pity, we meet Jephthah. He was a mighty warrior, but his mother was a prostitute. This was a stigma that he was never allowed to forget. His brothers had driven him away from his home and inheritance. He went to the land of Tob with a group of loyal followers. But when Israel needed a leader against the Ammonites the elders went crawling back to Jephthah (11:6–8). They promised to make him the ruler of Israel. Jephthah did not trust them, so he made them swear before God that they would keep their word. Then he led Israel to victory over the Ammonites.

With this in mind, what is the proper assessment of this man? Has Jephthah been defamed? There are two lines of evidence to consider, the same types of evidence considered by most courts of law: the evidence of the man's character and the evidence of the alleged crime.

Consider his character

Jephthah has a good character witness speaking for him, namely the Old Testament text. It is imperative that we hear what the book of Judges actually says and not the hearsay opinion of traditions and mistranslations. There are three parts of his character evidence that we need to think about: his band of men, his non-bitter spirit and his wisdom.

His band of men

Jephthah has been defamed because of the mistranslation of a word in 11:3. The NASV describes the sort of people who supported him: '... and worthless fellows gathered themselves about Jephthah, and they went out with him'. The RSV also calls them 'worthless fellows' whereas the KJV calls them 'vain men' and the NKJV has 'worthless men'.

In fact these are all prejudicial and unwarranted translations. The phrase used here (*anashim reyqim*, אֲנָשִׁים רֵיקִים) is neutral. It depends entirely on the context for its exact nuance of meaning. The basic idea behind the adjective (רִיק) is that of 'lightness', 'emptiness' or 'no value'. It does not imply an ethical idea. The word itself does not mean 'worthless fellow'. It is not a denigration of a man's character. If there are moral connotations, the context has to supply them. They do not arise from the word itself.

We saw an example of that in Judges 9:4 where the same word was used to describe the followers of Abimelech. There it does mean 'worthless' but only because of two things in the context. First, there is the unquestionably evil nature of Abimelech. Those who knowingly support a wicked man are tainted themselves. Second, the context immediately adds another word, 'reckless' (וּפֹחֲזִים), to explain the meaning of this 'lightness'. They were literally 'worthless and reckless fellows' (אֲנָשִׁים רֵיקִים וּפֹחֲזִים).

But there is nothing in the context of the Jephthah narrative to suggest anything like that about his men. Everything in the context suggests the opposite. They were brave men just like their leader, warriors of valour and courage, loyal to Jehovah and willing to die for him. Their loyalty to Jephthah indicated that they disagreed with the way that his family had treated him. Why should he unjustly bear the stigma of his mother's immorality? What could he do about it?

Therefore, correctly translated, these men were 'unimportant'. They were 'empty' or 'light on' in the sense of status, rank, importance[2] and pedigree, just like Jephthah himself. The NIV conveys the neutrality of the term by translating it as 'a group of adventurers'. They were just like the men who followed David at the cave of Adullam,[3] men of ordinary rank but extraordinary in valour and substance. Yes, Jephthah has been defamed and his colleagues with him.

His non-bitter spirit

Although he had been unfairly treated for the sins of his harlot mother and immoral father and put out of his home by his own brothers (who conveniently forgot that their father was the same man who used the prostitute), we do not find a bitter and twisted spirit. When the elders went cap in hand asking him to risk his neck and fight as their leader, he merely asked them to explain their changed attitude towards him: 'Didn't you hate me and drive me from my father's house? Why do you come to me now, when you're in trouble?' (11:7). This mild spirit is even more remarkable when you recall that the Mosaic Law forbids an illegitimate person like Jephthah (and his children) from ever joining in the assemblies of Israel for worship (see Deut. 23:2). This man never abandoned his love for Jehovah. He had a remarkable knowledge of covenant history and used it to help Israel as we will see in the next section.

Jephthah may well have been tempted to think that if he was not good enough to worship with them then he was not going to fight for them. But he did not. After issuing a due caution reminding Gilead's elders of their sins, he agreed to lay his life on the line as their leader. Commendably, he did not abuse his authority like Abimelech, taking revenge on his brothers. He respected the Law of God and joined the people of God and risked his life for the cause of God. Jephthah uses the name of Jehovah more frequently than any other character in the book of Judges and always in a proper and reverent way. He has undoubtedly been defamed.

His wisdom

Although he is described as 'a mighty warrior' (11:1), a man not afraid to fight, he knows that war should be avoided wherever possible. Therefore, he first tries to negotiate with the enemy. We should observe the skill of his arguments, revealing his accurate knowledge of (and belief in) the facts of covenant history. He asked what the king of Ammon had against Israel that he would attack them. The king answered, 'When Israel came up out of Egypt, they took away my land from the Arnon to the Jabbok, all the way to the Jordan. Now give it back peaceably' (11:13). Jephthah's wise answer has several elements to it.

1. Check your history
Your answer is wrong. When Joshua took the land it was not in your possession at all! Rather, Sihon the king of the Amorites had it (11:14–22).

2. Check your theology
Jehovah gave us this land as a gift:

> Then the LORD, the God of Israel, gave Sihon and all his men into Israel's hands, and they defeated them. Israel took over all the land of the Amorites … from the Arnon to the Jabbok and from the desert to the Jordan. Now since the LORD, the God of Israel, has driven the Amorites out before his people Israel, what right have you to take it over? (11:21–23).

Should we despise God's gift by giving it back to his enemies? Never!

3. Check your logic
You Ammonites are not the original settlers on this land either. You have no 'native title' claims at all! You attribute your settlement on that land to Chemosh your 'god'. You argue that the land is legitimately yours because you won it in battle, a battle where you claim that 'god' was on your side. You say that Chemosh fought for you. Why not allow us the same argument? We won it in

battle and we say that *Yahweh* was fighting for us: 'Will you not take what your god Chemosh gives you? Likewise, whatever the LORD our God has given us, we will possess' (11:24).

4. Check your calendars
It has been 300 years since we took over this disputed land, but during those three centuries you have done nothing to reclaim it. Why do you take action against us now? 'For three hundred years Israel occupied Heshbon, Aroer, the surrounding settlements and all the towns along the Arnon. Why didn't you retake them during that time?' (11:26).

After all of these good arguments Jephthah concluded: 'I have not wronged you, but you are doing me wrong by waging war against me. Let the LORD, the Judge, decide the dispute this day between the Israelites and the Ammonites' (11:27). But it fell on deaf ears so war was inevitable: 'The king of Ammon, however, paid no attention to the message Jephthah sent him. Then Jephthah went over to fight the Ammonites, and the LORD gave them into his hands' (11:28,32).

In summary, Jephthah was a man of knowledge, wisdom and courage. He was emotionally balanced. A rash person, as he is often described, would hardly have spoken so thoughtfully to his enemy in trying to avoid war. These are not the actions of a hasty, brash man.

Get on with your life! This is what we learn from Jephthah and his men. Jephthah did not let his unfortunate background mould his character or get him down. Yes, he was a social outcast, the son of a harlot, but he rose above it. He trusted God who sovereignly controls all events, including the family that you are born into, the wars that are fought and the lands that change occupation.

REMEMBER THIS

Beware of self-pity! Let us think like Jephthah. Let us not waste time bothering about things in the past that cannot be changed. Let our self-esteem come from our status in Christ not our status in the world. A mature outlook gets on with a useful godly life.

Consider his vow

Just two verses are devoted to the victory over Ammon (11:32–33). Much more attention is given to the vow. It is assumed that he vowed to make a human sacrifice, a burnt offering, the victim being the first person he saw coming out of his house after he returned from defeating Ammon. But the evidence is decidedly against this. As a challenge to the traditional approach three matters deserve our attention: the inconceivability, the dialogue with his daughter and the soft option refused.

How inconceivable!

Every Israelite knew that offering humans as a sacrifice by fire was an abomination to God. It is explicitly condemned in the Law in places like Leviticus 18:21, Leviticus 20:1–5 and Deuteronomy 12. Even when God tested Abraham, he did not allow Abraham to sacrifice his son. The burning of human sacrifices was typical of the idolatrous cult of Molech.

In Israel only specific animals were to be sacrificed at specific places by specific priests. In this context how could Jephthah vow to sacrifice a human? It is quite inconceivable that a God-fearing man would even think of such a thing.

It is even more improbable that he would think it would actually please God! There is no relief by claiming that Jephthah did not know the Law of God. Plenty of others did know it, so when he acceded to his daughter's request for two months before keeping the vow they would surely have told him, expressing their indignation. Let us take a closer look at the vow: 'And Jephthah made a vow to the LORD: "If you give the Ammonites into my hands, whatever comes out of the door of my house to meet me when I return in triumph from the Ammonites will be the LORD's, and I will sacrifice it as a burnt offering"' (11:30–31).

The problem lies in verse 31: '...*and* I will sacrifice it as a burnt offering'. It all depends on how you translate the letter *waw* (ו) placed in front of the verb. The first possibility is to translate it as 'or' ('*or* I will sacrifice'). The second possibility is 'and' ('*and* I will sacrifice').

The former deserves our support but it is very hard to find any English translation that uses it.[4] But it cannot be settled by grammar alone. The word is ambiguous because both meanings are possible. We have to appeal to the context. What makes the best sense, all other things considered? It seems that Jephthah is allowing for two different results. If it is a person that comes out the door he will consecrate them to the full-time service of God: '…whatever comes out of the door of my house to meet me when I return in triumph from the Ammonites will be the LORD's.' But if it is an animal, he will give it as a sacrifice: '…*or* I will sacrifice it as a burnt offering'. Anything else is inconceivable.

The dialogue with his daughter

> When Jephthah returned to his home in Mizpah, who should come out to meet him but his daughter, dancing to the sound of tambourines! She was an only child. Except for her he had neither son nor daughter. When he saw her, he tore his clothes and cried, 'Oh! My daughter! You have made me miserable and wretched, because I have made a vow to the LORD that I cannot break.' 'My father,' she replied, 'you have given your word to the LORD. Do to me just as you promised, now that the LORD has avenged you of your enemies, the Ammonites. But

grant me this one request,' she said. 'Give me two months to roam the hills and weep with my friends, because I will never marry.' 'You may go,' he said. And he let her go for two months. She and the girls went into the hills and wept because she would never marry. After the two months, she returned to her father and he did to her as he had vowed. And she was a virgin. From this comes the Israelite custom that each year the young women of Israel go out for four days to commemorate the daughter of Jephthah the Gileadite (11:34–40).

Jephthah was so upset that his daughter was the first to greet him not because he would have to put her to death to keep the vow but because he was going to dedicate her to full-time service in the Tabernacle at Shiloh, which meant that she would never marry. The text tells us why this was hard for Jephthah: it meant that he would have no descendants. His family line would cease with her: 'She was an only child. Except for her he had neither son nor daughter' (11:34).

There is a statement of result in verse 39 that is important to understand. Literally it says, 'At the end of two months she returned to her father, who did to her according to the vow which he had made; and/so she had no relations with a man.' It tells us that the result of Jephthah fulfilling his vow is not that his daughter died but that she remained a virgin. There is no mention of her death, but three times the text mentions her virginity. The vow committed her to celibacy.

A telling point in Jephthah's favour is the attitude of his daughter. She showed great respect for her father and for God by insisting that the vow be kept even though it removed many of her freedoms. There are no innuendoes against his character. From her home this girl has learned a godly morality and respect for her earthly father and her heavenly Father. She had been raised by a father who set a good example for her. Whatever his faults, he was not a rash, wild, headstrong or foolish man.

He refused the soft option

There was a way out of the vow, a soft option for Jephthah. According to the Law of Moses (Lev. 27) many avowed things could be redeemed or paid out in money. The first 8 verses deal with people who had been vowed (Jephthah's situation). The person pledged had a cash value assigned to them by the priest and that money was paid so that the person could go about their normal life. We have to assume that Jephthah knew about this law. If he did not one of his friends could have told him about it on seeing his misery. But he did not take the soft option because, as a God-honouring man, he knew that God sees the intention of the heart. Jephthah exemplifies Psalm 15:4: '…who keeps his oath even when it hurts.' His yes meant yes.

Has Jephthah been defamed? The evidence points that way. However, the vow is open to valid criticism in two other aspects. First, he was bargaining with God, saying in effect that if you do this for me, I will do that for you. Second, it was unfair because it was too general. He pledged *anything* or *anyone* without knowing whose rights and privileges would be affected. It is one thing to pledge *yourself*; it is quite another thing to commit someone else without his or her prior consent. It is not defamation to admit these faults in Jephthah.

QUESTIONS FOR DISCUSSION

1. How serious is it to wrongly impugn a man? (See Exod. 20:16; 23:1; Prov. 6:16–19; 8:7; 12:17; 17:15; 19:5; James 4:11; 1 Peter 2:1.)

2. Does the Bible support character testimony as a valid appeal? (See John 10:37–38; 14:10–11; Titus 2:7–14; 1 Peter 2:12; 3:8–17; James 2:14–24.)

3. 'High service requires a lowly mind.' Assess this statement in light of Psalm 84:10; Psalm 131; Luke 1:46-53; Romans 12:3–8; 1 Corinthians 1:25–29; and 2 Corinthians 4:5–7.

THE GUIDE

CHAPTER TWELVE

WHAT ABOUT SAMSON? (PART 1)

THE GUIDE

BIBLE READING

Judges 13–16

LOOK IT UP

INTRODUCTION

Samson is one of the most puzzling, enigmatic and even bizarre characters in the whole Bible. One moment we find him tearing a lion apart with his bare hands then he is tying 300 foxes together in pairs at the tail with flaming torches between them. Next he is swinging the jawbone of a donkey and killing 1,000 men with it. Then, after leaving a harlot's house at midnight, he performs an astonishing feat of strength unequalled by any athlete since. He ripped up the fortified city gates of Gaza, pulled its two great posts clean out of the ground, along with its heavy metal bars, hoisted the whole lot onto his shoulders and carted it many miles uphill to the top of a mountain near Hebron. Perhaps he dumped it there as a defiant signal that he would come back to ruin the Philistines.

In the face of such things we naturally ask, What about Samson? He is such a dichotomy. One moment he is acting very foolishly and the next he does great things for the kingdom of God. How are we to evaluate him?

Samson is the major judge in the book of Judges. Four chapters are devoted to him. It is wise to treat the Samson narrative in two stages. The first priority concerns the correct approach for biblical interpretation. There are three useful questions to help us do this:

1. Is Samson in heaven?
2. Is Samson naturally strong?
3. Is Samson a type of Christ?

Is Samson in heaven?

A lot of sincere people have pondered this question: Is Samson in heaven? Is he a saved man? This question arises because Samson's sins and faults, including sexual immorality, are openly mentioned in the text. The common tendency is to approach Scripture moralistically. This approach assumes that the writer lists all the events in Samson's life for us to condemn him when he does wrong and applaud him when he does well.

If we approach Samson's life moralistically we might think the following: 'Samson is marrying a woman of Timnah, a Philistine. He is marrying outside the church, being unequally yoked. *Tut-tut! Don't do that!* Samson is at a harlot's house: *he shouldn't do that!* And look, Samson is tying foxes together. *How cruel! Call the humane society!* And now Samson is in bad company. *Beware of Delilah, bad company corrupts good morals!* No wonder we see Samson getting his eyes gouged out

— *beware your sins will find you out.* He married someone who was right in his own eyes (14:2–3) and now he loses those eyes in judgement!'

When all these moral assessments are totalled Samson does not have a good record, and we wonder if he will be in heaven after all. But this is not the way to interpret Scripture. The inspired writers did not compose their books to expose the faults of men like Samson to induce us to register our disapproval. Whether the moral lessons are right or wrong is irrelevant to the issue of correctly interpreting this book.

The correct framework for approaching Scripture is covenantal. The Bible describes the covenant acts of God in history, working mightily in his chosen people. They are people with true faith, yet they are ordinary, sinful people who belong to God's covenant community. If we take this broad covenantal view we will discover that moralizing about Samson makes us miss the point. We miss the big picture in our distraction with side issues. Unfortunately the moralistic approach leads to the conclusion that Samson is a negative example and not a positive one. Samson then becomes an anti-hero instead of a hero of faith.

But the New Testament says the opposite. The book of Hebrews, in which mention is made of Samson, takes a broad covenantal view of the Old Testament. Its priests and sacrifices, its kings and judges and the Exodus and promised land are all interpreted covenantally, not moralistically. What does it say about Samson? It regards him as eminently fit for heaven, a hero of faith (Heb. 11:32), a great champion of the covenant and an example of faith in action. Although not perfect, his life is truly characterized by allegiance to God and by courage and covenant keeping.

If we have never seen Samson in this light before we have never seen him the way that the New Testament does, the way that God sees him. Will Samson be in heaven? Most certainly, as will Moses, Abraham, Noah, Gideon, Samuel and David and all the heroes of faith. Let us look at the covenantal approach another way. Suppose the Bible devoted four chapters to your life and laid bare many of your sins rather than Samson's. How good would you look? Would we wonder if you were going to heaven? Would you have even half the good things that Samson had going for him?

The moralistic approach is wrong. Every true believer goes to heaven on the basis of God's gracious covenant, which is realized and fulfilled in Jesus Christ. This is exactly how Samson gets to heaven. The next chapter shows significant evidences of Samson's faith. As we will see, if there is any finger of moral blame, the author points it mainly at Israel, not Samson.

Is Samson naturally strong?

What is your mental picture of Samson? Do you picture him as a 'Mr. Universe' rippling with muscles or a puny

WHAT THE TEXT TEACHES

weakling? Do you picture Samson as right at home in the gymnasium, pumping iron and causing onlookers to marvel at his robust physique? If you were an artist, how would you draw him? Would he look like a heavyweight boxer or a reserve in the croquet club?

These questions expose an implied error. Samson is usually pictured as a man of great natural strength, but the book of Judges disagrees, and it disagrees plainly and repeatedly. Samson's strength is not natural. The following great acts of strength done by Samson are due to the power of God through the Holy Spirit:

- 'The Spirit of the LORD came upon him in power so that he tore the lion apart with his bare hands as he might have torn a young goat' (14:6).
- 'Then the Spirit of the LORD came upon him in power. He went down to Ashkelon, struck down thirty of their men, stripped them of their belongings and gave their clothes to those who had explained the riddle' (14:19).
- 'The Spirit of the LORD came upon him in power. The ropes on his arms became like charred flax, and the bindings dropped from his hands. Finding a fresh jawbone of a donkey, he grabbed it and struck down a thousand men' (15:14–15).

When he performed his ultimate act of power (pulling down a Philistine temple and killing many godless mockers), Samson made it very clear where his strength came from: 'O Sovereign Lord, remember me. O God, please strengthen me just once more' (16:28).

The fact is that Samson was an ordinary man. The text says nothing about Samson's physique. He may well have been a small man with a puny physique. However, the more we cater to his physical appearance, the more we take credit away from where it is due — the Spirit of God! His strength was not natural but supernatural. He was not conscious of being born with unusual strength. He could never have performed such feats until the Spirit of God came mightily on him. Notice how the writer introduces him with all this in mind: 'The woman gave birth to a boy and named him Samson. He grew and the LORD blessed him, and the Spirit of the LORD began to stir him while he was in Mahaneh Dan' (13:24–25).

The lion attack

Samson was on his way to Timnah (14:1–6). He got as far as the vineyards of Timnah when suddenly a lion came charging on him. According to verse 5 it was 'a young lion', or more exactly, 'a savage young lion' (אֲרִיוֹת כְּפִיר). Therefore, it was at the peak of its lethal strength. Its teeth and claws were sharp and strong. Moreover, the text literally says that Samson 'had nothing in his hand' (וּמְאוּמָה אֵין בְּיָדוֹ) (14:6). He was completely unarmed. What was in his mind at that moment?

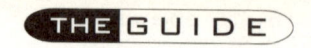

THINK ABOUT IT

It would be reasonable to assume that Samson was terrified like any normal man. Unarmed men do not survive the attack of a savage lion. But suddenly something happened that had never happened to him before — the Spirit of God rushed mightily on him. Divine power overwhelmed Samson, and he found himself doing something that only God could enable him to do — something that he would never have believed — ripping a lion apart with his bare hands!

We should not be surprised to read: 'But he told neither his father nor mother what he had done' (14:6). Why not? For a start, who would believe it? Even showing them the lion's dead body would still leave them sceptical, wondering why Samson was not mauled or even scratched. Presumably Samson himself was utterly amazed. Such a stunning event would not be easy to rationalize in his mind. One thing he did know: supernatural power had gripped him giving him a foretaste of how God was going to use him to deliver Israel from the Philistines. What we see here is God commissioning Samson, starting him off in the work ahead of him. God empowered Samson to save himself from a lion as a token that he would empower Samson to save Israel from the Philistines.

Samson's strength was not in his muscles — it was miraculous. Until that day he had never experienced such strength before. It did not come from the gymnasium. So this is not just 'history' in Judges: it is covenant history — God at work! From this point onward Samson's strength was connected to his faithfulness to God.

The Philistines

Samson's determination to marry a Philistine girl was unsuccessfully resisted by his parents (14:2–3). The author immediately adds an interpretive insight: 'His parents did not know that this was from the LORD, who was seeking an occasion to confront the Philistines; for at that time they were ruling over Israel' (14:4). This is not an endorsement of Samson's decision. The Mosaic Law made it clear that Israelites were not to marry Gentiles.[1] His parents were absolutely correct to challenge his disobedience: 'Isn't there an acceptable woman among your relatives or among all our people? Must you go to the uncircumcised Philistines to get a wife?' (14:3). The author does not disagree with them.

His intention is to remind us of God's secret purposes. God rules and overrules in all events. God will use even Samson's disobedience as an occasion for advancing his covenant plans. It is not only Samson's parents who 'did not know that this was from the LORD'. None of us can ever know the secret will of God. It is not our concern. As Moses made clear, we are to be guided by his revealed will: 'The secret things belong to the LORD our God, but the things revealed belong to us and to our children forever, that we may follow all the words of this law' (Deut. 29:29).

The writer makes no attempt to hide Samson's weakness in matters of sexual morality (though he does not dwell on it either): 'One day Samson went to Gaza, where he saw a prostitute. He went in to spend the night with her' (16:1). Presumably we are expected to disapprove of this. Indeed, we are inclined to think that Samson is about to get what he deserves: 'The people of Gaza were told, "Samson is here!" So they surrounded the place and lay in wait for him all night at the city gate. They made no move during the night, saying, "At dawn we'll kill him"' (16:2).

But Samson thwarted their plans, leaving his calling card in a most defiant manner: 'But Samson lay there only until the middle of the night. Then he got up and took hold of the doors of the city gate, together with the two posts, and tore them loose, bar and all. He lifted them to his shoulders and carried them to the top of the hill that faces Hebron' (16:3). Again we need to remember the writer's interpretive clue. Behind the actions of Samson the Lord was at work delivering Israel from the Philistines (see 'A lone-ranger man' in chapter 13). The voluntary activities of men (both sinful and virtuous) will ultimately accomplish God's sovereign purposes. None of this justifies immorality but it does demand a covenantal interpretation of history.

Even though the episode with Delilah (16:4–20) brings shame to Samson it is clear that God was still prepared to use him. Three times Samson toyed with her, pretending to divulge the secret of his strength. Each time, when the Philistines were on him, his God-given strength delivered him. He became more reckless, and his response to Delilah's third interrogation came dangerously close to revealing his solemn commitment to God as epitomized in his Nazirite vows: 'If you weave the seven braids of my head into the fabric on the loom and tighten it with the pin, I'll become as weak as any other man' (16:13).

It is truly pathetic that such a mighty warrior would fall for Delilah's final speech: 'How can you say, "I love you," when you won't confide in me?' (16:15). No doubt it was accompanied with all the pouting and fawning that a deceitful lover could turn on. We are not specifically told Delilah's nationality. Although her name is Semitic, she was clearly Israel's enemy, a Philistine through and through. We are left in no doubt about her relentless persistence: 'With such nagging she prodded him day after day until he was tired to death' (16:16).

So Samson gave in, revealing his Nazirite obligations. But not for a moment did he feel vulnerable. Though he was tempting God and presuming on grace he was very confident. When Delilah again forecast his defeat, Samson thought: '"I'll go out as before and shake myself free." But he did not know that the LORD had left him' (16:20). This time Samson was humiliated: 'Then the Philistines seized him, gouged out his eyes and took him down to Gaza. Binding him with bronze shackles, they set him to grinding in the prison' (16:21).

No attempt should be made to justify Samson's actions here. But, as the next verses show, Samson rose above this ignominy to deliver Israel yet again. He had not finished serving the Lord, and God had not finished using Samson. The Lord had left him temporarily (and justly so). The author's next comment is far more than a mere cosmetic observation: 'But the hair on his head began to grow again after it had been shaved' (16:22). It encourages our hope that Samson might yet be restored. We anticipate that *Yahweh* might still be pleased to deliver Israel through him. In this context it is an outward indication of an erring Nazirite renewing his commitment to God. Samson was about to perform the greatest saving act of his life. In a mode typical of Christ, Samson was about to defeat more enemies in his death than he ever did in his life.

Is Samson a type of Christ?

In the world of computers a *true type* is a scaleable printing font. The standard (default) font has its own size, shape and proportion. However, being a true type it can be reproduced in an enlarged or scaled-up form without any distortion, irregularity or loss of proportion.

In the world of biblical studies a true type is a scaleable Old Testament person, event or institution. It first appears and has its meaning (in default mode) in its original historical-cultural environment (its own size, shape and proportion). But God 'scales it up' later on. He causes the true type to be expanded so that it stretches beyond its original default setting but without loss of proportion. The original person, event or institution is repeated in some larger form in connection with Christ and his kingdom. A *type* (like Noah's flood) depicts an *antitype* (judgement day when Christ returns). So 'typology' is the technical theological term for someone or something that stands in for another. Is Samson typical? Is Samson an example of a larger paradigm? Is he a type of Christ?

The answers are positive. Samson is typical of Christ, the ultimate Saviour. All the judges, including Samson, are typical because they collectively point to Christ. Just as the *priests* collectively point to Christ and his sacrifice and the *kings* and *prophets* point to Christ's rule and word, the judge-deliverers point to the great Judge-Deliverer. This is true of Samson perhaps more so than any other judge. Why is that? Two suggestive lines of thought will help us.

The unexpected

First, consider 'the unexpected' element. Samson saved Israel in quite unexpected ways. It is a feature of the judges as a whole. Indeed, it features in covenant history as a whole. Who would have expected God to deliver Israel by parting the Red Sea? Who would have anticipated manna falling from heaven, flocks of quail blowing into camp or water gushing from a rock?

WHAT THE TEXT TEACHES

Shamgar's oxgoad was certainly an unorthodox weapon, not to mention Gideon's strange little army with clay pots and torches. Who would have predicted the instrumental role of women in defeating two of Israel's worst foes? Jael used a tent peg to kill Sisera, and a woman threw an upper millstone onto Abimelech. If 'unusual' is the order of the day then Samson excels.

Samson's victories involved him swinging the jawbone of a donkey, bursting ropes apart, setting fiery foxes loose in Philistine crops, telling riddles and dumping the city gates on top of a mountain. But then again, who would have expected the Messiah to save his people by dying as a condemned man? The Jews expected the very opposite, a military conquest by a mighty warrior king marching to victory before a helpless Roman empire, restoring Israel to the highest place on earth.

REMEMBER THIS

Scripture prepares us for the unexpected. God's ways are not our ways. The Jews should have been well prepared for the unexpected, but they were not. Their history should have shown them that God's methods of deliverance are unique, amazing and far higher than our ways. Samson's story is very typical of salvation being achieved in a way that men would not have expected.

Powerful in death

Consider also the theme of 'powerful in death'. When Samson died by pulling the Philistine temple down, what was the interpretive clue? It lies in the writer's comment: 'Samson said, "Let me die with the Philistines!" Then he pushed with all his might, and down came the temple on the rulers and all the people in it. Thus he killed many more when he died than while he lived' (16:30). Samson's greatest victory came in his death. He hurt the covenant enemy more in his courageous death than he did in his courageous life.

What could be more typical of Jesus Christ than this? Although his life and works were wonderful, it was Christ's death on the cross that achieved the greatest victory. There he died, as it were, with the Philistines but not as a Philistine! There he pulled down the temples of this world signalling the imminent destruction of all false religion. There in his death is *the death of deaths*. There is the serpent crushed, the grave robbed of its sting and the curse of condemnation removed from every believer. Surely we must say of both Samson and Jesus that they were most triumphant over the enemy in their death. It can be said of each of them: 'Thus he killed many more when he died than while he lived' (16:30).

Yes, Samson will be in heaven. But what about you? Are you in covenant with God? Are you typical of saved people? Has the Holy Spirit ever come on you giving you new birth? What Samson did to the Philistines is only a faint picture of what Christ will do to his enemies on the last day. But if we are true believers we are as safe as Samson. The same powerful Spirit of God strengthens us. May we all own the salvation freely offered in the gospel.

QUESTIONS FOR DISCUSSION

1. *How do the following texts show the danger of moralizing? (See Ps. 130:3; Rom. 3:9–24; Gal. 3:10–14; Eph. 2:8–9; Titus 3:4–6.)*

2. *Christ's return at the end of the age involves some expected and unexpected elements. Identify them both in Matthew 24:30–25:13 and 2 Peter 3:1–14.*

3. *'Not only Samson, but all God's people are empowered by the Holy Spirit.' Evaluate this statement using John 3:1–8; 14:16–18; Romans 8:1–11,13–17; and 1 Corinthians 12:1–13.*

… THE GUIDE

CHAPTER THIRTEEN

WHAT ABOUT SAMSON? (PART 2)

BIBLE READING

Judges 13–16

Samson was an amazing saviour who wreaked havoc on the Philistines. The basic principles for properly interpreting him have been established. As we proceed to build on those foundations the following three ideas will help us to correctly understand Samson:

1. A lone-ranger man
2. A faithful man
3. A misunderstood man

A lone-ranger man

There was no army! Samson saved Israel by himself, a solo champion against the Philistines. He did not have the 10,000 warriors available to Deborah and Barak. He did not even have the 300 men of Gideon's army. He defended God's covenant and kingdom as a real 'lone ranger'. In fact everyone else in Israel appeared to be content with Philistine rule. They were used to it by now.

The reason that Samson did not lead an army of Israelites is that no Israelite army could be found. No one was willing to fight. To that extent this is the lowest point of Israel's history in the three centuries covered by the book of Judges. Samson is God's man in the darkest days. He was denied the support enjoyed by previous judges. Worse, Samson's kinsmen actually wanted to stop him fighting for their salvation!

The Philistines did not realize what they were starting when they burned Samson's wife and father-in-law (15:6–8). Samson took his vengeance by slaughtering many of them. This incited reprisal: over 1,000 Philistines came and camped in Judah to hit back at Samson. The staggering fact is that the local Israelites took sides with the Philistines! No less than 3,000 men of Judah decided to act as agents of the enemy. They set out to capture Samson and hand him over to the Philistines. They said to Samson, 'Don't you realize that the Philistines are rulers over us? What have you done to us? ... We've come to tie you up and hand you over to the Philistines' (15:11–12). What they were saying was: The Philistines rule us and we are happy for it to stay that way. Why are you disturbing this arrangement? You are the problem Samson not them!

If the finger of moralizing is to be pointed anywhere, let it not be pointed at Samson but at those faithless, covenant-breaking Israelites. Such treachery against the God-given leader is a paradigm of Judas Iscariot. Samson was *the* man of God in Israel — the only one of courage and faith. He was the one fulfilling the prophecy of the angel of the LORD: 'And he will begin the deliverance of Israel from the hands of the Philistines' (13:5).

THINK ABOUT IT

From a covenant point of view, the Philistines posed a worse threat than all their other enemies. Why? They allowed considerable freedom for Israel. They permitted intermarriage (even Samson married a Philistine). The Israelites had a great degree of freedom to travel and mix in the Philistine society. But therein lay the problem and the seeds of Israel's death. If this continued, the covenant line of Israel would be wiped out. The Messianic line would be absorbed into paganism. This spiritual and cultural seduction was far more dangerous than the harsh oppression from Israel's other enemies. The devil is far more dangerous when we feel comfortable with him.

Samson was God's solution to this emergency. His task was to remove the comfort zone. He agitated and troubled the deadly peace. He had to be a 'lone ranger' because no one else could see the real issues. Israel was comfortable with the devil. So Samson's job was to keep the Philistines at bay, to make things hard for them. He stopped the church from becoming a mere suburb of the world. And what a champion he was! The Philistines became so preoccupied with trying to capture this one man that they deployed thousands of soldiers over a long period, but they were unable to consolidate their rule over Israel any further. Samson held them in check, single-handedly, for twenty years until the battle of Mizpah when Samuel was finally able to raise an army and end Philistine rule (1 Sam. 7:7–13).

This is the light in which we should understand Judges 13:25: 'and the Spirit of the LORD began to stir him while he was in Mahaneh Dan, between Zorah and Eshtaol.' Because God was using Samson alone on behalf of the back-slidden Israel, he gave him unique provisions of power and strength. The writer's one moral judgement is not against Samson but against Israel: 'Again the Israelites did evil in the eyes of the LORD' (13:1).

A faithful man

Several admirable qualities of Samson's faith and godliness are often overlooked. An example is seen in his gracious and exemplary treatment of the 3,000 traitors. Samson's own kinsmen were willing to support the enemy and betray their only hope of salvation. Here was their chance to get behind him and form an army and act as brave men of God. They had seen clear evidence that God's hand was on this amazing deliverer. Presumably they had heard about the lion attack. They would certainly have known about how Samson killed thirty Philistines and took away their clothing (14:19).

WHAT THE TEXT TEACHES

They also would have known about the foxes as well as Samson's slaughter of many in revenge for the murder of his wife.

But despite the proof of his prowess, these 3,000 Israelites came to hand Samson over. Even the fact that 3,000 men came to get him, not just five or ten, shows that they were convinced of his amazing ability and strength. You do not normally send 3,000 police officers to arrest one man living in a cave!

Samson would be justified in dealing severely with these pathetic cowards. But he was gracious. He merely said to them, 'Swear to me that you won't kill me yourselves' (15:12). He was willing to be tied up firmly with two new ropes without frays or weak spots. Samson believed that God was still with him and that he would soon snap the ropes like cotton threads. So why did he make them promise not to kill him? Was he afraid of death? Nothing in the context would imply this.

THINK ABOUT IT

Samson had their safety in mind! Samson had work to do, and if these Israelites tried to stop him from doing what God had commissioned him to do, he would have to fight *them* first. How would they stand against such a charismatic spirit-empowered warrior? In the following verses he stands triumphantly against 1,000 Philistine warriors killing them all with a piece of bone. He could certainly do a lot of damage to these 3,000 Israelites, and they knew it. Why else would they send 3,000 men to capture him? His 'do not try to kill me' really meant 'do not make me kill you'!

Notice also his courageous approach to the enemy. He trusted God to strengthen him at the critical moment. Bound with two new ropes meant that escape was impossible by human means. There he was delivered into the hands of thousands of cruel enemies baying for his blood, the lone Israelite who had taunted, harassed and defeated them long enough. When they saw him coming in bonds they broke out shouting, thinking that they had him! But this is Samson, the man of God and hero of faith. He burst the ropes like flax melting in flames. Seizing the nearest thing he could find, the fresh jawbone of a donkey, he hurled himself into battle. Not one of the 3,000 Israelites lent a hand or gave him a word of encouragement as he slew 1,000 servants of the devil.

Samson attributed the victory to God: 'He cried out to the Lord, "You have given your servant this great victory"' (15:18). He admits to being the mere instrument and gave God the glory as the real source of the power and the victory. This man is not proud or arrogant; he is essentially God honouring. It is time that we recognized Samson for his courage and godliness.

God clearly showed his approval of his servant. Samson had thoroughly exhausted himself in the Lord's work, proving that real human effort was involved in deploying his supernatural strength. The Holy Spirit did not bypass Samson's humanity. Therefore, wearied from battle, Samson prayed for a refreshing drink. The Lord's response is marvellous, not only in giving Samson a drink but in emphatically registering divine approval. God provided a miracle, creating not only a one-time drink but also a perpetual spring that flowed with water for a long time afterward. It became known in Israel as *En Hakkore*, 'the spring of him who called'. It was a monumental reminder for generations of Israelites that Samson was God's faithful man.

He was also a true martyr. The narrative climaxes with Samson at his weakest point. His hair is gone, his eyes are gouged out and he is shackled in bronze chains, enslaved by the Philistines. We see him being led about by a young boy as the Philistine hordes make sport of him. They gathered to see this former great warrior humiliated, to spit, mock and rail at him in his moment of weakness. This is another reminder of Christ, whom Samson typifies.

But this was the hour of Samson's greatest faith and victory. Whatever his sins of the past, he is not paralysed by remorse and guilt. He has presumably repented, and what we see is not a man bowed down in disgrace but a hero of faith, a man zealous for God. He is sizing up the situation and sensing yet another opportunity to do battle for the kingdom of God and to win another victory over the enemy of Israel.

Understandably there is an element of retributive justice in his demand: 'Let me with one blow get revenge on the Philistines for my two eyes' (16:28). But remember, Samson is supposed to take vengeance! He is the civil magistrate in Israel. He is the arm of the law. But there is far more than justice here. The real contextual clue is religious. Samson could hear the Philistines defying *Yahweh* and giving glory to the idol god Dagon: 'Now the rulers of the Philistines assembled to offer a great sacrifice to Dagon their god and to celebrate, saying, "Our god has delivered Samson, our enemy, into our hands"' (16:23).

So Samson prays to the one true God using three distinct names: 'Then Samson prayed to the LORD (*Yahweh*), "O Sovereign Lord (*Adonai Yahweh*), remember me. O God (*Elohim*), please strengthen me just once more"' (16:28). Here is the prayer of a martyr who, for the sake of honouring God, is prepared to die: 'Let me die with the Philistines!' (16:30). Samson is saying that if saving your people requires my death, so be it! This was Christ's attitude on the cross also. It was Samson's finest hour: 'Thus he killed many more when he died than while he lived' (16:30). Jehovah triumphed that day, not Dagon, and the man who made that very obvious was Samson.

A misunderstood man

Samson is misunderstood in a number of areas. Some of these have been noted already but two more deserve

WHAT THE TEXT TEACHES

thoughtful attention. The first concerns his Nazirite vows. God commanded Samson's mother that he was to be a Nazirite from birth (13:5). This means that he was dedicated to God and separated from various normal liberties of life. The outward tokens of a Nazirite included refraining from cutting the hair, drinking wine and touching a dead body (Num. 6). Samson eventually broke the vow by telling Delilah about the cutting of his hair. But it is frequently alleged that he broke his vow much earlier in two separate incidents.

The first was when he took honey from the carcass of the lion, thereby touching a dead body. Thus it is claimed that Samson was unfaithful right at the start of his time as a judge. But this is not so. The actual language used in Nazirite vows seems to refer only to dead humans, not animals. The term used is *nephesh*, which means 'soul'[1] (Num. 6:6). Moreover, exactly the same prohibition applied to the priests (Lev. 21:11). Obviously it did not refer to dead animals because the priests were constantly in contact with dead animals in the ritual sacrifices. Both priests and Nazirites were permitted to touch dead animals without breaking their vows.

The second incident refers to the seven days of festivity at Samson's wedding. It is claimed that he drank wine, the normal beverage at weddings, and worse, that it was the influence of drink that led Samson to wager thirty sets of clothing on a riddle: 'Out of the eater, something to eat; out of the strong, something sweet' (14:14). But this is an argument from silence, which is easily answered.

If Samson broke his vow by drinking wine, why did he not lose his strength there and then? He certainly lost his strength when he broke his vow regarding the cutting of his hair. So why should one form of violation count, whereas another form of the same sin does not? If a vow is broken, it is broken. The precise manner of how it was broken is a mere detail. Samson has been misunderstood. Every indication is that he was faithful to his vows throughout his entire period as a judge: more than twenty years. It was only near the end of his life that he failed by telling Delilah his vow. Samson has suffered a lot of damage from critics who make hasty, unfair allegations.

Samson has also suffered unjustly over the incident with the foxes (15:4–8). Any allegation of 'cruelty' seems to be based on several misconceptions. Should we assume that each pair of tails was literally knotted together and pulled tight? This is very unlikely. How would the foxes then be far enough apart to run freely in the same direction? The text simply says, 'he tied them tail to tail in pairs' (15:4), meaning that he tied them at the tail end. The idea of tying two together is probably to prevent any fox escaping down a hole — two tied together could not coordinate such an exit! The most likely scene is that a cord was used to join each pair of foxes, perhaps with a few feet of slack between each fox.

Some have assumed that the burning torches harmed the foxes. The text suggests nothing of the sort. It was against Samson's interests to harm the foxes. His aim was to have them run widely through the Philistine crops, setting fire everywhere. The fire was kept well away from the foxes so that they could run all day without harming themselves. Therefore, it is most likely that another piece of cord was dragged between each pair of foxes, attached to a burning oil-soaked rag. As they ran it would skip across the ground, setting fire to the standing grain, the piles of cut grain and the vineyards and olive groves.

What we see here is an amazing feat by a God-equipped warrior. What other man could do such a thing? Let the challenge go out worldwide: catch 300 wild foxes single handed then join them in pairs tail to tail! We see here a hero of the covenant displaying remarkable skill and wisdom against God's enemies. It was a brilliant method for one man to cause maximum damage as he delivered Israel from the Philistines.

Look at Samson covenantally and see a real hero of faith! Seen in a covenantal context Samson prefigures Christ. If Samson has been misunderstood so has Christ. If Christ is not your Lord and God, you have certainly misunderstood him. By the grace of God put it right today!

QUESTIONS FOR DISCUSSION

1. *What factors make treachery so painful? (Read Ps. 41; Matt. 26:14–25, 47–50; Matt. 27:3–5.)*

2. *If Satan is entirely evil, what makes it so easy for anyone to be comfortable with him? (See Gen. 3:1–5; Matt. 7:15; 2 Cor. 11:14; 1 Thess. 2:1–12.)*

3. *If Christ is the ultimate Samson, who is the ultimate Philistine? (See Matt. 12:22–32; John 3:16–21; Rev. 22:12–21.)*

THE GUIDE

CHAPTER FOURTEEN

FINAL FLASHBACKS

BIBLE READING

Judges 17–18

The last five chapters of the book of Judges are flashbacks. This section is an appendix, where the writer takes us back over the moral, political and social life of Israel by describing two incidents: the first in chapters 17 and 18 and the other in chapters 19 to 21. There are several things to notice about these chapters.

Although they are placed at the end of the book they do not follow chronologically after Samson. In fact the evidence suggests that these incidents belong to the earliest years in the period of the judges. For example, we are told: 'In those days the ark of the covenant of God was there, with Phinehas son of Eleazar, the son of Aaron, ministering before it' (20:27–28). Moses was still alive when Phinehas became the high priest (Num. 25), and Joshua had not yet led them into the promised land. So the historical setting of these final flashbacks is very early.

The writer's purpose was to show us the terrible corruption and unfaithfulness in Israel. But instead of simply telling us that the situation was very bad he makes it vivid by describing two actual events, leaving us to draw our own conclusions. We are shocked that these wicked things are being done, not among the pagan nations but among God's people. Worse, it happened as soon as they received their inheritance, the promised land. These flashbacks show us just how quickly and extensively sin can spread. They show us just how difficult the task was for the various leaders (judges).

The purpose of these flashbacks is moral. We are meant to draw moral lessons from them. This might sound paradoxical because the danger of approaching Scripture in a moralistic way has been emphasized. Is this contradicting the covenantal approach? No, because the writer specifically indicates that he is teaching moral lessons. He is warning us about disobedience.

He does this by means of an important comment: 'In those days Israel had no king; everyone did as he saw fit' (17:6). This comes as his summary explanation of the first incident of a son who robs his mother, and she in turn robs God. This comment becomes a virtual chorus. The book closes with it ringing in our ears: 'In those days Israel had no king; everyone did as he saw fit' (21:25). These identical statements are important markers at the beginning and end of this final section of the book. They are the interpretive keys. And, to make it more obvious, the writer reminds us twice more in between these two points: 'In those days Israel had no king' (18:1; 19:1).

THINK ABOUT IT

There is a big difference between *moralistic* interpretation and *moral* interpretation. These real-life descriptions are the writer's way of telling us what happens when people live as they please! We are to look at these flashbacks and learn the moral lessons they so plainly teach. There is nothing here to contradict a proper covenantal approach to the Bible. The covenant includes important moral obligations for God's people. Disobedience amounts to covenant breaking! By picking up the writer's clues we are learning lessons about faithfulness to the covenant and the terrible consequences of refusal.

As we turn to the first part of his appendix, the author relates three incidents. One concerns a man named Micah and his mother, the next is about a Levite and the third is about the tribe of Dan. They reveal corruption at all levels of Israelite society: private corruption (at the family level), official corruption (at the religious level) and tribal corruption (at the social level).

Private corruption (family level)

Judges 17 introduces us to a grim family scene set in the hill country of Ephraim. It involved a man named Micah and his mother. Micah robbed his mother of 1,100 pieces of silver. To get an idea of the value, we are told that the yearly wage he paid his Levite was 10 pieces of silver plus accommodation: 'Then Micah said to him, "Live with me and be my father and priest, and I'll give you ten shekels of silver a year, your clothes and your food"' (17:10). So Micah stole the equivalent of 110 years wages! He robbed his own mother of a fortune! But when he heard her cursing the unknown thief it got the better of him and he gave the money back: 'The eleven hundred shekels of silver that were taken from you and about which I heard you utter a curse — I have that silver with me; I took it' (17:2).

And what did his mother say? She neither rebuked him nor blamed him. She made the sort of pathetic comment we still hear from mothers of criminals today, mothers in a state of denial: 'The LORD bless you, my son!' (17:2). Why this pathetic denial of criminality? Because she was exactly the same — a thief who dishonoured God! How do we know this?

The writer tells us: 'When he returned the eleven hundred shekels of silver to his mother, she said, "I solemnly consecrate my silver to the LORD for my son to make a carved image and a cast idol. I will give it back to you"' (17:3). She promised to consecrate all the 1,100 shekels of silver to God. But she lied. The next verse records that she paid out only 200 shekels. What happened to the other 900? She kept it. She thought that lying to God was a trivial thing. Here is an Old Testament example of the same sin recorded in

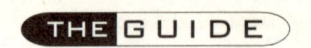

Acts 5, where Ananias and Sapphira were struck dead for lying to God. They also pledged money but cheated on their promise (Acts 5:3–5).

But her indulgence got worse. After lying to God she also led her son into open idolatry. Micah used the 200 shekel's worth of graven images to establish a fully-fledged shrine in their home: 'And they were put in Micah's house. Now this man Micah had a shrine, and he made an ephod and some idols and installed one of his sons as his priest' (17:4–5). This is especially heinous for an Israelite. It is completely against the Mosaic Law. The word 'shrine' is literally 'house of gods'. This private shrine was complete with an ephod (priestly garment), molten images, graven images, and portable household idols called teraphim. And if that was not bad enough, Micah wanted his own personal priest, so he ordained his son into instant priesthood.

Family life had so degenerated in Israel that people stole from their own flesh and blood. They were liars, idol worshippers and hardened and perverse against *Yahweh* their God, to whom they owed everything. The writer shocks us even further by asserting that this was not unusual, not untypical: '...everyone did as he saw fit' (17:6). This was not an isolated incident. It was commonplace in Israel in the days before the kings.

Shiloh, the place of worship, was also in the hill country of Ephraim, the same area as Micah's house. Therefore, Micah did not make the shrine because the distance was too far for him to travel in order to worship God lawfully. He made the shrine because of sheer disobedience to the word of God.

The shrine was undoubtedly very lavish and beautiful. It seems to have become a tourist attraction because it caught the eye of the travelling Danites who stole its contents for themselves. But beautiful or not God hated it. It was repugnant to God. Homemade gods are a blatant denial of the infinite God who made the universe! This sin is still common today. Churches have become shrines, buildings full of expensive idols and images and man-made treasures. They are still tourist attractions. Crowds flock to see them. The Vatican treasures displayed in Brisbane during 'Expo 88' included images of Mary and the saints. They are venerated and bowed down to and kissed and prayed over. They are no less repugnant to God than Micah's idols.

THINK ABOUT IT

Trivial gods are loved by trivial minds. When the Danites saw that Micah was upset after they stole his idols, they asked: '"What's the matter with you that you called out your men to fight?" He replied, "You took the gods I made, and my priest, and went away. What else do I have? How can you ask, 'What's the matter with you?'"' (18:23). Here is a fool whimpering over his homemade gods. How pitiful these gods are if you have to both make and protect them![1]

What a warped sense of values! Micah had no qualms about robbing the true God of his glory but as soon as anyone takes away his useless homemade deaf and dumb idols he becomes very offended and goes whimpering to get them back. Like Abimelech's warped sense of values, afraid to die with the reputation that a woman killed him, Micah was pathetically fixated on lost idols.

Official corruption (religious level)

The Levites were a special group in Israel, set apart to assist Aaron and his sons in the ceremonial worship of God. They had no inheritance in the land but instead were sustained by the tithes and gifts of the rest of the people. They were allocated certain designated cities to live in (Num. 35:1–8; Josh. 21:20–40). Levites were a perpetual reminder of God's mercy when he spared the firstborn of every family. So the Levites were people with a special role, special privileges and special significance in Israel. If anyone should have been faithful to God it was the Levites. But this was not so.

In this flashback we meet a young Levite from Bethlehem. To begin with, he should not have been there. Bethlehem was not one of the cities designated for the Levites. But he was an opportunist looking for work that suited him. He was a man dissatisfied with God's arrangements for his life. He came to Micah's house, and his 'house of gods' impressed the Levite. When two men with no real respect for God get together sin multiplies. Micah wanted a priest and made the Levite an offer too good to refuse.

For a while he seemed content but then a committee of five Danites visited them. They asked this false priest to inquire of God for them, to see if their plans would prosper. He obliged them by telling them what they wanted to hear: 'Go in peace. Your journey has the LORD's approval' (18:6). Later they returned with 600 armed warriors and stole Micah's idols. The Levite, seeing his source of employment being taken away, protested: 'What are you doing?' (18:18). But he was offered another promotion if he went with them (18:19). So he left Micah and climbed the corporate ladder and became priest of all the Danites.

Again this is not an isolated instance. At the start of the story (17:6) and in the middle of it (18:1) the writer says that there was no king and no authority being heeded. Everyone was pleasing themselves. On reflection this scene is familiar to us. How often in history have men in the church been corrupted by favours, prestige and promotions within the system?

Tribal corruption (social level)

Judges 18 begins with the tribe of Dan still looking for a place to call home, which was entirely their own fault. They had been allocated a very rich area (Josh. 19:40–48), but they refused to trust God and never drove out the Amorites. As a result, they were forced out of the rich valleys and into the hill country (Judg. 1:34). Tribes like Dan were paying the price for their unfaithfulness (Judg. 2).

Instead of obeying God they went looking for a comfortable place where the native people were unprepared, undefended and vulnerable. They found it in the far north at Laish — a quiet area colonized by some Phoenicians, isolated from any allies. So they decided to make Laish their home (18:7–11). They were disobeying God. Corruption was widespread — the whole tribe of Dan was implicated. No wonder they did not go to Shiloh to ask the true priest of God about God's will. They already knew God's will and were avoiding it. Instead, they went to Micah's 'priest' and got the guidance they wanted.

The extent of their corruption is seen in the stealing of Micah's idols (18:18–26). We might be tempted to dismiss this. After all, they are just vain idols, and Micah should not even have them. But this is still theft, and look how insensitive to crime the Danites were! They said to Micah, 'What's the matter with you...' (18:23). What is a bit of theft between neighbours? They demanded his silence and threatened to murder him and his household. What callous, wicked hearts for a tribe of God's people! This was the state of Israel in the time of the judges.

These flashbacks reveal the sort of community that the judges worked in. Theirs was no easy task. One of the valid lessons to be drawn from all of this is that there is nothing new about paganism in the church. When church people backslide they do not necessarily become complete atheists or irreligious sceptics. In some ways it would be better if they did. But few people entirely abandon their religion. They tend to cling to traditional things, but it is purely nominal and ritualistic. They reject biblical standards. They change the meanings to suit themselves. Micah still worshipped but only by using idols. He still had a priest but one of his own making. The meanings of words change, but the same words are used. Paganism gets into the church through pagans who stay in the church. Words like 'faith', 'resurrection' and 'revelation' are still used but entirely wrong meanings are applied to them.

We should also observe how sin hardens people. Sin makes men blind and presumptive to a staggering degree. It is evident in the brazen confidence of Micah. Surrounded by his idols he said, 'Now I know that the LORD will be good to me, since this Levite has become my priest' (17:13). He was outwardly very religious and very confident yet grossly offensive to God. The more we sin the more hardened we become. As if anesthetized, a hardened sinner is in a painful state but cannot feel it. Like Micah he may even feel euphoric but feelings are no guide to right and wrong.

We can see why the book of Judges was necessary. It was preparatory for the next stage of the covenant: the kingdom period. God intended to give Israel a king who would rule in a completely godly way.[2] Some of the kings of Israel approximated that ideal but not perfectly.

As an institution the kings pointed to Christ — the true King — the perfect man who rules according to all of God's will. Unless we are in his kingdom and under his rule we are rebels by definition. Unless we are true Christians we are doing what is right in our own eyes. May God grant us the grace to always be loyal to King Jesus and not to live as we please!

QUESTIONS FOR DISCUSSION

1. What is the difference between art and idolatry? (See Exod. 20:4–6; 25:18–20; 32:1–14.)

2. Evaluate the following statement: 'Images of God are always lying images'. (See Deut. 4:10–19; Gen. 1:26–27; 9:6; Ps. 106:19–21; Isa. 40:18; Hab. 2:18; 2 Cor. 4:4; Col. 1:15; James 3:9.)

3. Does ignorance excuse the heathen? (See Ps. 19:1–4; Isa. 44:6–21; Rom. 1:20–23; 2:9–15.)

CHAPTER FIFTEEN

NO KING — DO ANYTHING!

BIBLE READING

Judges 19

The scene before us is not a pretty sight. It confronts us with such repulsive things as homosexual depravity and gang rape. Sadly, Judges 19 easily typifies our situation today. Our society has grown tolerant and supportive of deviant behaviour. Tolerance for homosexuality is now regarded as a mark of sophistication and enlightenment. This same tolerance helped to destroy the Roman Empire, and our text shows that it existed in the ancient Near East over 3,000 years ago. Far from being sophisticated or enlightened it remains a very crude and ancient depravity.

No king — do anything! That is what it was like in the time of the judges — anything goes! Four times the writer tells us that it was so. And now he confronts us with three sad realities of the moral depravity of homosexuality. It was 'baptized sodomy', wilful sodomy and cursed sodomy.

'Baptized sodomy'

The nineteenth chapter in Judges is reminiscent of the nineteenth chapter in Genesis, which describes the abominations of Sodom and Gomorrah. But this time it is even worse because Sodom and Gomorrah were pagan cities, whereas Gibeah was an Israelite town. Sexual perversion is disgraceful anywhere but when it exists among the people called by God's name it is repugnant to the highest degree.[1] It was *'baptized sodomy'* because it was condoned and performed by God's chosen people.

Judges 19 tells of a Levite who had a concubine (a second-class wife). She left him, returning to her father, so the Levite came to retrieve her. Her father was very hospitable, effusively so, and it became difficult for them to leave without appearing ungrateful. But they eventually left late one afternoon, reaching Jebus (Jerusalem) in the evening. It was a Gentile city so they did not stay there but passed on to Gibeah in the Israelite territory of Benjamin. The custom was for travellers to go to the town square where locals could see them and offer hospitality. But no one bothered. They would have spent the whole night in the open square except for one kind person, an old farmer coming in from a day's work.

As they were sitting down at dinner, enjoying the old man's company, a horrible thing happened. A mob of homosexuals started beating on the door, shouting for the old man to bring out the Levite for them to sodomize: 'Bring out the man who came to your house so we can have sex with him' (19:22).

The old man's protest was an odd mixture of strength and weakness. To his credit he did rebuke them for such vile intentions: 'The owner of the house went outside and said to them, "No, my friends, don't be so vile. Since this man is my guest, don't do this disgraceful thing'" (19:23). It took a lot of courage for an old man to go outside and face a mob of wretches like that. But his courageous speech was inherently weak.

THINK ABOUT IT

It seems that the rampant immorality in Gibeah had hardened even this old man. He implicitly granted some concessions. Rather than being ethically based, his argument was purely circumstantial: 'this man is my guest' (19:23). But what if he had not been a guest? What if he was a local citizen? This 'situation ethic' argues that it is wrong to sin in this situation, but it might be right in different situations. His rebuke should have been the moral absolute — 'Don't be so vile!' (19:23). The almighty God condemns sodomy. It is an abomination in every situation.

This observation does not deny that even true believers can backslide, falling into sinful ways (like drunkenness or lust). Stronger believers should help them out of it rather than write them off but without indulging their weakness. The moral absolutes still apply. Whatever medical or social factors might explain their lapse, they do not justify or mitigate them.

But his next words knock the wind right out of our sails: 'Look, here is my virgin daughter, and his concubine. I will bring them out to you now, and you can use them and do to them whatever you wish. But to this man, don't do such a disgraceful thing' (19:24). What a dreadful statement from any old man, let alone an old man in Israel! It is exactly the same concession made by Lot in Genesis 19. In effect he says: *I will not allow homosexual gang rape against men but gang rape against women... that's different, that's okay. I'll even provide the victims for you!* What dreadful inconsistencies in this man's ethics. He suggested that they divert from one sort of abomination to another. We can hear the author's theme coming through again: 'In those days Israel had no king; everyone did as he saw fit' (17:6). No king — do anything!

When he could see that the frenzied mob would not listen, the Levite seized the woman he supposedly *loved* and tossed her out into the street, where they abused her all night long. The Levite found her in the morning lying at the doorway — that was as far as she managed to crawl. Without a tear of remorse or any show of affection he simply said to her, 'Get up; Let's go.' But she was dead.

This is a thoroughly sickening incident. Imagine how abhorrent it must have been to the almighty God, the Holy One! It would be naive to brush this aside as mere ancient history, as if the Christian church is not like that today. It is common knowledge that some churches refuse to condemn sodomy. It is no longer unusual to read stories of churches worldwide 'marrying' two homosexuals and sending them on their way with a benediction. Here in Queensland the *Joint Churches Social Justice Commission* supports the decriminalizing of private adult homosexual acts and not only holds that godless opinion but has taken pains to persuade the *Criminal Justice Commission* to change the law in favour of sodomy.[2]

What a lewd and filthy harlot the 'church' has become in some places today. True believers must lift up their voices in protest and warn the church of its sins. Some churches have 'baptized sodomy' by welcoming practicing homosexuals to the Lord's Table. The message that this communicates is undeniable: *Go and do your abominations with our blessing, with God's blessing, and we welcome you to the Lord's Table to eat the bread and drink the cup in memory of Christ, until he comes again.* Satan's work is being done by the church! May God keep us from a guilty silence.

Wilful sodomy

Homosexuality is a choice not a sickness. It is a deliberate perversion. The proof is obvious. Here was a mob of homosexuals who preferred the man, the Levite, but when they could not satisfy their evil appetites with him they settled for the woman. It is a false but common claim that homosexuals cannot help being what they are and doing what they do. It is a lie to say that they cannot be blamed, that it is natural for them and it is the way that they were born! The text shows that in this situation these men were quite capable of heterosexual acts and when they chose homosexual acts it was a deliberate choice.[3]

Where does the homosexual choice come from? We need to be quite clear on the answer because homosexuals are very militant, spending millions of dollars promoting themselves as good members of a society that has unfairly judged them. They lobby governments with considerable success. For many years now governments in Australia have granted money to homosexuals and lesbians. They are winning recognition in law as legitimately married in same-sex relationships. They claim to be suitable parents to adopt and nurture children, and they demand the same respect as that given to normal family units. They even have their own 'churches'!

This is all thoroughly contrary to the Bible. Romans 1 tells us why people become homosexuals. Sodomy is first a religious choice and then it becomes a sexual choice. The Bible says that sodomy is the result of a deliberate choice to deny God, to swap truth for a lie, to suppress the truth in unrighteousness and to worship the creature rather than the Creator:

> They exchanged the truth of God for a lie ... Because of this, God gave them over to shameful lusts. Even their women exchanged natural relations

for unnatural ones. In the same way the men also abandoned natural relations with women and were inflamed with lust for one another. Men committed indecent acts with other men, and received in themselves the due penalty for their perversion (Rom. 1:25–27).

It is only God's restraining grace that prevents any of us from degenerating into degrading behaviour patterns. The problem is spiritual. Men choose to reject God and that is ultimately why they choose to be homosexual. God does not force them or cause them to do what they would rather not do. He gives them up to do what they choose. God is not the author of evil. They can never blame God for their sodomy by saying that they cannot help it, and that God made them that way. The only way to avoid these straight facts about sodomy is to call God a liar to his face!

If any further evidence is needed Romans 1:28 provides it: 'Furthermore, since they did not think it worthwhile to retain the knowledge of God, he gave them over to a depraved mind, to do what ought not to be done.' Homosexuality is the consequence of a depraved mind. It shows what happens when God gives men over to themselves. It is obvious why true Christianity is the great enemy of homosexuality. The real answer to homosexuality is spiritual. There must be repentance, confession of sin, faith in

Christ for forgiveness and a cessation of the godless behaviour.

Because of the heat that this subject generates, some caveats are in order. We need to keep some other truths in mind to avoid simplistic thinking. We should not assume that each individual homosexual has consciously gone through the steps described in Romans 1, which describes the 'macro-process' for humanity as a whole, not the 'micro-process' for every individual. Undoubtedly for many, homosexuality is a learned behaviour pattern and is often the result of rejection or abuse that they have suffered themselves. Tragically we are discovering that some people learned it through being abused by leaders within a religious organization. So homosexuality is not necessarily simple to explain.

REMEMBER THIS

We should also avoid victimization. We should not single out homosexuality for more attention than any other sin. Yes, it is an 'abomination',[4] a word that God reserves for only a select number of especially heinous and hideous sins. But it is not incurable or unforgivable. The gospel hope offered to liars, idolaters, slanderers, cowards, traitors and thieves is the same hope offered to homosexuals.

We must also avoid being naive. It is unrealistic to assume that all traces of the problem will disappear the moment that a person becomes a Christian. The fact is that some believers can struggle with homosexual feelings for the rest of their lives. We need to realize that there are ex-homosexuals who have become true Christians and entered into normal marriages. Although they no longer commit homosexual acts they still struggle with some of the scars of their old way of life. Help is available, and our privilege as fellow Christians is to steer them to that help and to provide the mature, genuine love and acceptance that will strengthen them.

Notwithstanding, homosexuality is never to be excused, condoned or cosmetically sanctified. It is an utter abomination. It is not 'gay'. We need to resist the massive flood of propaganda against the biblical position. Words like 'homophobic' are completely out of order. They are part of the propaganda aimed at discrediting the Bible's teaching as mere fanaticism and paranoia. There is a right and proper fear of immorality. There is a right and proper fear of all godless sinful things. Those who have no fear of sexual depravity only advertise the barren state of their soul! If murder was given legal protection in society, many would be afraid. Would that sane fear be dubbed 'murderophobic'?

It is not harsh and unloving to stand firm on these truths. Christians are the only people who can ultimately help homosexuals. We are the only people who know the cause of the problem and the cure for it! Once we reject what God says in Holy Scripture, we cut them off from the truth and from any hope of salvation. And then we too have blood on our hands. Homosexuality is not natural. The apostle Paul described it as *impure, degrading, unnatural, indecent, depraved, improper* and *inflamed with lust*. It is our duty to uphold the truth.

Cursed sodomy

Homosexuality is incompatible with Christianity! There is no such thing as a *homosexual Christian*. The two words are mutually exclusive. A homosexual is one thing: a Christian is another. But due to gullibility and ignorance large sections of the visible church deny it. They believe that you can simultaneously have a grossly perverted, abominable and degrading private lifestyle and yet be a loving disciple of Jesus Christ.

A Christian with a homosexual lifestyle is just as impossible as a Christian with a drunken lifestyle or a Christian given to theft, idolatry, superstition, blasphemy or witchcraft. They are mutually incompatible courses of life. That is precisely what the Corinthians needed to learn:

> Do you not know that the wicked will not inherit the kingdom of God? Do not be deceived: Neither the sexually immoral nor idolaters nor adulterers nor male prostitutes nor homosexual offenders nor thieves nor the greedy nor drunkards nor slanderers nor swindlers will inherit the kingdom of God.

And that is what some of you were. But you were washed, you were sanctified, you were justified in the name of the Lord Jesus Christ and by the Spirit of our God' (1 Cor. 6:9–11).

You cannot be an heir of God's kingdom and a homosexual at the same time! However, it is possible to be an ex-homosexual who is now a Christian. That was exactly what some of the Corinthians were. But the proof of their Christianity was their change of habits. They were washed, cleaned and sanctified: such *were* some of you not such *are* some of you. The Ephesian church was told exactly the same truths: 'But among you there must not be even a hint of sexual immorality, or of any kind of impurity, or of greed, because these are improper for God's holy people' (Eph. 5:3). Do not be deceived into believing anything different! Sodomy is cursed: Christianity is blessed. Between them there is no neutral ground.

Judges 19 forces an important conclusion on us — make no concessions to sexual wickedness. Both the old farmer and the Levite made that mistake. They were prepared to countenance sexual wickedness in one form but not in another. Our society is making big concessions to sodomy, and sadly some professing churches are also. These churches have allowed them to be church members in good standing, allowed them to come to the Lord's Table, ordained them for pastoral ministry, condoned living together in sodomite marriages and regarded their lifestyle as a safe and loving environment for training children.

If God had reason to bring painful judgement on Israel, he has no less reason to judge the modern church. Let us uphold the chaste, clean and God-given sexual privileges of a husband and wife in marriage. Let us warn people that every other sexual union is godless. May numerous homosexuals learn these truths and turn to the living God, finding the same cleansing and forgiveness available to all. And may they in turn take the amazing grace of Jesus Christ to others still lost in degradation. We must never cave in to unbiblical standards: 'You are the salt of the earth. But if the salt loses its saltiness, how can it be made salty again? It is no longer good for anything, except to be thrown out and trampled by men' (Matt. 5:13).

QUESTIONS FOR DISCUSSION

1. *What is the connection between 'love' and 'truth'? (See 3 John 1–11.)*

2. *'Immorality can never be excused.' Is this an exaggeration? (See Lev. 18:21–30; 1 Cor. 5:1–13; Eph. 5:3; Rev. 21:8.)*

3. *How does immorality undermine the gospel? (See 1 Cor. 6:15–20; 1 John 3:3–10; Jude 3–4.)*

THE GUIDE

CHAPTER SIXTEEN

A STITCH IN TIME

BIBLE READING

Judges 20

One of those self-evident truths we all acknowledge is the proverbial saying: 'A stitch in time saves nine.' A problem ignored is a problem increased. It becomes more widespread and deeply entrenched. Judges 20 is awful proof of this. An army of 400,000 men was now needed to fix the problem in Israel. A complete tribe (Benjamin) was decimated. It was a very costly 'nine stitches', leading to a whole new set of problems (described in Judges 21). 'A stitch in time saves nine':

1. It was true for them
2. It is true for us

It was true for them

A summary of the issues in Judges 20 will help our understanding. The story begins where the previous chapter ended, repeating the grim facts about the Levite cutting up his concubine's dead body into twelve parts. Messengers delivered these grisly tokens, one piece for each of the twelve tribes. It was similar to the method Saul used for rallying the whole nation to war (1 Sam. 11:1-8), except that he cut up the body of an ox into twelve parts.

They all knew how to interpret the message. It was a call for discipline. It demanded that the problem in Gibeah be ignored no longer: 'Everyone who saw it said, "Such a thing has never been seen or done, not since the day the Israelites came up out of Egypt. Think about it! Consider it! Tell us what to do!"' (19:30). They knew that some drastic action would be needed. It would be unpleasant and people would be hurt, but there was no option. So they debated their procedure.

They all assembled at Mizpah to carry out the long overdue discipline. No less than 400,000 gathered 'as one man' (20:1,8,11), armed for battle and intent on the death penalty for the men of Gibeah. However, one tribe was missing — Benjamin. Benjamin refused to take action. Gibeah was part of their tribe, and instead of weeding out the culprits from their midst they closed ranks, showing the same misguided loyalty that has so often hindered the church in exercising discipline. However, the eleven united tribes vowed not to return home until justice was done: 'All the people rose as one man, saying, "None of us will go home. No, not one of us will return to his house"' (20:8).

Benjamin was foolish in harbouring criminals. It is simply dishonest to support and protect guilty people, whether they are friends or family. It is ungodly to show such bias and partiality, but it often happens in the church. We can never help anyone by granting them asylum from the consequences of their sins. True friends are those who hold us accountable for our actions.

THINK ABOUT IT

Benjamin's misplaced loyalty greatly hindered the course of justice. Because the tribe lived in the hill country, it was much easier to defend than attack. To get to them was literally an uphill battle. Their obstinacy ensured a lot more damage than was necessary. They refused to cooperate with due process. They intended to fight all the way regardless of the facts. Sadly it is not unknown for church courts (like presbyteries) to be hindered from carrying out biblical oversight when congregations close ranks to protect the guilty.

We are told that Benjamin's warriors were dangerous fighters. Apart from 26,000 swordsmen, they had 700 left-handed men 'who could sling a stone at a hair and not miss' (20:16). These were their marksmen or snipers, all crack shots! The slings are not to be confused with the slingshots once common among schoolboys for firing small projectiles like marbles. They were true weapons of war used by the Assyrian, Egyptian and Babylonian armies of the day. It has been estimated that a proficient warrior could project stones weighing as much as one pound with great accuracy at speeds of ninety miles per hour. David proved it when he killed Goliath.

Aware of this, the assembly made careful plans for a protracted civil war, allocating 40,000 men (ten per cent of the troops) as the food supply line for those fighting in the front line (20:10). Thus prepared they demanded that the tribe of Benjamin hand over the guilty people. But they refused: '"Now surrender those wicked men of Gibeah so that we may put them to death and purge the evil from Israel." But the Benjamites would not listen to their fellow Israelites. From their towns they came together at Gibeah to fight against the Israelites' (20:13–14).

What a curse when congregations show misplaced loyalty, granting asylum to their guilty friends. The increased bloodshed is all on their hands. And what terrible bloodshed there was. As usual, there were casualties on both sides. Innocent people were hurt by misguided loyalty. The rest of the chapter describes the carnage. There were three separate battles before the end of the war.

In the first battle God selected Judah as the first tribe to fight (20:18–23). This conflict only lasted for half a day but very heavy losses were sustained — 22,000 being slain. Naturally they asked the Lord if they should persist in such a difficult case and God insisted: 'Go up against them' (20:23).

In the second battle the assembly of Israel was humiliated in defeat again, losing 18,000 men (20:24–28). But there was a change of attitude. They not only shed tears (as on the first day), but they also fasted and made sacrifices. They recognized the need for God's help. Merely going through the right procedures and steps of discipline is not enough. This time the Lord not only sent them out, but he promised victory: 'Go, for tomorrow I will give them into your hands' (20:28).

Having learned twice that a direct frontal attack did not work, they changed tactics for the third battle (20:29–36). Knowing that the Benjamites were now confident to the point of arrogance, they planned a pincer movement to take advantage of their attitude. They would lure them out of their strongholds and ambush them from both front and rear. It was the same method used by Joshua at the battle of Ai (Josh. 8).

It was a successful move and terribly so. Only 600 men escaped from the entire tribe of Benjamin: 'But six hundred men turned and fled into the desert to the rock of Rimmon, where they stayed four months' (20:47). This raised a whole new set of problems. How would this tribe survive? As we will discover in the last chapter, it led Israel to act pragmatically, doing sinful things in order to find wives for Benjamin's 600 men so that the twelve tribes could continue.[1] One fact is undeniable: a problem ignored is a problem increased. 'A stitch in time saves nine.'

It is true for us

It is useful to cite a few modern illustrations of how this principle applies to both known and potential problems. The following scenes are actual situations experienced in the course of pastoral ministry. They show what happens when a church is unwilling to learn the lessons of texts like Judges 20. If we do not learn the lessons of the past we are bound to repeat its mistakes.

THINK ABOUT IT

We can learn from the garden! Failure to weed the garden early means that little weeds grow bigger and more numerous. Small weeds can be removed easily without even disrupting the soil, but once established they are hard to remove. Larger tools are needed, a certain amount of good soil is lost, clinging to the weeds, and some bad seed is unavoidably scattered, giving birth to a new set of problems in the future.

Case 1: known problems

There was once a viable Australian congregation that was reduced to just one family of about six people. A boy, well known for stealing, had begun molesting other children in the church. Parental complaints were ignored and the church did nothing about it. The minister refused to deal with the problem, and the elders would not deal with it. Some years later a different minister found out about the immorality in the church, and he began the biblical steps of discipline. But, like Benjamin of old, the Session closed ranks because the boy's father was one of the elders. The matter then came to the presbytery, but it also refused to deal biblically. Why? The boy belonged to a church family of long standing. Missionaries and ministers had come from that family.

The presbytery gave a mere token of discipline, a verbal rebuke to the boy, but it was so inadequate that the minister and elders left (all except the boy's father). The whole congregation left in disgust except the members of that one family. The church never recovered. The point is that failure to act early decimated a whole congregation! Even if the one early stitch of discipline is unpleasant it must be done to avoid the far greater unpleasantness that will inevitably follow. 'A stitch in time saves nine.'

Case 2: potential problems

The same lesson applies to problems gathering on the horizon like dark clouds. Hindsight is not needed when reasonable minds sense a storm brewing, as it was in the 1960s. Ordinary Christians were struggling to cope with several related issues. The scholarly discipline of manuscript studies had made significant progress in the preceding century, resulting in a proliferation of new Bible versions. Some were reasonable, but others were not.

Some were paraphrases rather than translations and should never have been packaged as 'The Bible'. Some put too much emphasis on the targeted audience. Their excessive 'dynamic equivalence' produced something that was easy to read but not very accurate. The worst examples reflected religious prejudices inimical to key gospel truths, such as Christ's virgin birth and substitutionary atonement. It was not hard to see a potential storm brewing, especially in conservative churches.

The storm hit with devastating consequences in the late 1970s. As you would expect many sincere Christians were concerned about which Bible translation to use. Some versions caused disquiet as readers saw liberties being taken with the true text of Scripture. They were horrified to see the word 'virgin' changed to 'young woman'. They rightly sensed a hidden agenda when a key term like 'repentance' was reduced to 'sorrow' and 'propitiation' was downgraded to 'the remedy for our defilement' (like a tube of ointment or a course of antibiotics). A stitch in time was urgently needed. Churches needed to guide their people. Those with a good knowledge of the theological issues and proper principles of translation should have informed Christians of the strengths and weaknesses of all the new translations.

The storm in one denomination (the Presbyterian Church of Eastern Australia) had three discernible stages. At first, people adopted the practical view that the safest policy was to retain the old King James

Version (KJV). After all it had a good track record, serving the church well since 1611. A commonly expressed view was that if the old Bible was trustworthy then, it is still trustworthy now.

However, reactions quickly moved into a dangerous second stage where the KJV was given an exaggerated status. It was now *enshrined* rather than merely retained. It was now promoted as the *best* translation. It soon became the symbol of orthodoxy, the *sine qua non* of faithfulness. If you carried any Bible except the KJV you were suspect! Some congregations (officially or unofficially) banned all other versions from the pews, the lectern and the pulpit. A dangerous polarization took place. The motto 'KJV only' was widely promoted. Simplistic books, with titles like *God only wrote one Bible* (J. J. Ray, Eye Opener Publishers, 1976), added fuel to the fire.

Then the final stage arrived. What had begun as a healthy fear of *bad* translations had grown into a full-blown paranoia against any *new* translations. One minister who epitomized this view published a book called *Mountains of Myth*.[2] His view so divided his church that he was dismissed from the ministry. He taught that the KJV was without mistake or error in translation. He claimed that the English text was not inferior to the Hebrew and Greek originals, being 'mediately' inspired by God.

This minister could not read a word of Hebrew or Greek, yet he asserted that the KJV translated every bit of the original languages with infallible accuracy! He convinced a group of people who naively followed him. His doctrine of Scripture was, of course, truly heretical. It was contrary to the truth that he had vowed to uphold in the *Westminster Confession of Faith*. After a traumatic discipline case lasting some years the minister was removed. Several congregations were severely affected, families were divided and unfounded rumours were rife. Nipped in the bud the problem would never have been so serious.

Let us learn the lesson of Judges 20. We need to be alert to both existing problems and potential problems in ourselves, in our families and in our churches. The first signs of trouble should be dealt with immediately. If not we will become desensitized and tolerant of sin.

An exhortation is appropriate for church leaders responsible for dealing with difficult situations where a 'stitch in time' was neglected. Do not be surprised to see Benjamin's behaviour repeated today! Do not be surprised when tribal allegiances make your job harder because congregations or groups of people close ranks behind the guilty. Recognize it as the sin it is!

Church members often have a false sense of honour and a misguided sense of loyalty. They support their guilty friends, ministers and elders included. They close ranks. They act on sheer emotion and lose the ability or the willingness to see and think straight. They get very bitter and will turn on anyone trying to bring biblical remedies to bear. Press on! Truth must prevail.

Expect intimidation! Guilty people often resort to it when they are forced to give account. They love to threaten church governments with lawsuits. Of course we must always act wisely and lawfully. But we must also act courageously. If God is for us, who is against us! Truth is so precious that it has no place in the hands of cowards. Even if we are threatened with a lawsuit we must continue doing the King's business.

Although the Israelites lost two battles and many casualties, the Lord told them to press on to victory. Let us regard sin in ourselves and in the church as the unwelcome and polluted thing it is, and let us clean up the mess! A stitch in time does save nine.

QUESTIONS FOR DISCUSSION

1. *How does Scripture view human partiality? (See Lev. 19:15; Deut. 1:17; 2 Chr. 19:7; Prov. 17:15; 24:23–26; 28:9,21; Ps. 82:2–4; Eph. 4:25; 1 Tim. 5:21–22.)*

2. *How do Proverbs 24:30–34 align with Judges 20?*

3. *What principles for church discipline are implied in the following texts? (See Prov. 1:7; 3:11–12; 5:22–23; 10:17; 12:1; 13:18,24; Heb. 12:5–11; Rev. 3:19.)*

THE GUIDE

CHAPTER SEVENTEEN

LEGALISM TO THE RESCUE!

BIBLE READING

Judges 21

Legalism is a very crafty sort of sin. Basically, legalism means *using the Law in order to avoid the Law.*[1] A legalist strains at what the law *says* in order to avoid doing what the law *requires*. The Pharisees were expert legalists. Jesus exposed their zealous attention to matters of legal minutiae while they ignored the weightier matters of compassion, love and justice:

> Woe to you, teachers of the law and Pharisees, you hypocrites! You give a tenth of your spices — mint, dill and cummin. But you have neglected the more important matters of the law — justice, mercy and faithfulness. You should have practiced the latter, without neglecting the former. You blind guides! You strain out a gnat but swallow a camel (Matt. 23:23–24).

The Sermon on the Mount is our Lord's famous dismantling of their legalistic interpretation of God's laws on adultery, murder, oaths and vows and many other matters. Fallen man is ingenious at legalism, at finding loopholes and technicalities in the law in order to defend illegalities. Australian legalists have produced some clever 'bottom of the harbour' schemes designed to cheat on taxation laws. Hardly a month goes by without revelations of more corporate corruption schemes that, though technically plausible, are contrary to the very intent and purpose of the law.

In the last chapter of the book of Judges we see Israel resorting to legalism as a way out of a difficult situation. Legalism to the rescue! Because it has practical applications for us, we will consider legalism in Israel and legalism in the church today.

Legalism in Israel

The problem that faced Israel in Judges 21 was the imminent extinction of the whole tribe of Benjamin. Only 600 men were left after the long overdue discipline described in chapter 20. There were no surviving women or children. The obvious solution for rebuilding Benjamin was for the men to find wives from the other eleven tribes. But they had taken vows to prevent that: 'The men of Israel had taken an oath at Mizpah: "Not one of us will give his daughter in marriage to a Benjamite"' (21:1).

But this proved to be unwise. Hindsight made them regret such a rash and excessive policy. It put them in a real bind.

> 'With the women of Benjamin destroyed, how shall we provide wives for the men who are left? The

Benjamite survivors must have heirs,' they said, 'so that a tribe of Israel will not be wiped out. We can't give them our daughters as wives, since we Israelites have taken this oath: "Cursed be anyone who gives a wife to a Benjamite"' (21:16–18).

What could they do to solve this problem? They resorted to legalism. They thought of a way to break their vows without appearing to do so, a way of getting around the law without breaking the letter of the law. They found and exploited two legal loopholes.

First, they thought of a way to exploit another 'law'. They had made a vow that anyone who failed to assemble at Mizpah in the battle against Benjamin should be put to death (21:8–9). As it happens, no one had come up from Jabesh Gilead (on the east bank of the Jordan). So they sent 12,000 warriors to carry out the vow. They executed all the men, women and children there, with the convenient exception of 400 virgins among them. They were given as wives for the men of Benjamin. This legalism had a clever plausibility.

It really boils down to a semantic legal definition of the word 'us' in the vow: 'Not one of us will give his daughter in marriage to a Benjamite' (21:1). To justify themselves they argued that they had not broken the first vow! None of us gave our women as wives for Benjamin. We gave the daughters of Jabesh Gilead. Because Jabesh

Gilead was not present when the vow was made, strictly speaking they were not a party to it, so the law did not forbid the daughters of Jabesh Gilead from becoming wives to the men of Benjamin.

Moreover, for those who want to be pedantic, the vow says, 'Cursed be anyone who gives a wife to a Benjamite' (21:18). If anyone deserves the curse it is the people of Jabesh Gilead because they refused to join in the fighting. By giving their virgins as wives for Benjamin, we solve two problems at once and keep two vows at once. Benjamin is saved from extinction and Jabesh Gilead is cursed for its cowardice. Legalism to the rescue!

A second loophole was found because they still needed another 200 wives for Benjamin. So they thought of a way to exploit another word in their vow, the word 'give': 'Not one of us will give his daughter in marriage to a Benjamite' (21:1). The ingenious plan is described in verses 19 to 24. It was the annual festival at Shiloh. Each year the local girls would come into the open fields and dance with joy to the Lord. It was probably part of the feast of Tabernacles. It would be easy for 200 hidden men to wait for the right moment to grab a girl and take her home to marry. Israel promised to turn a blind eye if the men of Benjamin were to kidnap 200 girls from the festival, which is what happened:

> So they instructed the Benjamites, saying, 'Go and hide in the vineyards and watch. When the girls of Shiloh come out to join in the dancing, then rush from the vineyards and each of you seize a wife

from the girls of Shiloh and go to the land of Benjamin. When their fathers or brothers complain to us, we will say to them, "Do us a kindness by helping them, because we did not get wives for them during the war, and you are innocent, since you did not give your daughters to them"' (21:20–22).

When the men of Shiloh come to complain about this kidnapping we will have a good answer ready. We will defend your actions and show how necessary they were. We will show them how law-abiding we all are. None of us have broken the law. We all kept our oath. None of us actually gave wives to Benjamin. On the contrary, the Benjamites took the women so technically we are all keeping to the letter of the law and solving a problem at the same time.

Despite the ingenuity it was sheer legalism. The whole aim and intention of the vow was that wives from the eleven tribes would not be supplied for Benjamin under any circumstances. Of course the correct and honourable solution was for them to repent of those vows. They were reckless, unnecessary, excessive and bloodthirsty. They went far beyond the justice and discipline deserved by Benjamin for harbouring the sinners in Gibeah.

> **REMEMBER THIS**
>
> Repentance is a hard pill to swallow. Repentance means that we admit our wrongdoing, confess it and turn from it, seeking God's forgiveness and making restitution to victims as far as possible. It is the only honourable and proper way to deal with our sins.

Why are men legalists? Why do they seize on semantic details and milk every drop out of technicalities? Why argue from silence using what the law does not say to get around what it so obviously does say? The answer is left ringing in our ears in the final words of the book: 'In those days Israel had no king; everyone did as he saw fit' (21:25).

This means that legalism is evidence of a lawless heart. It is an attitude of unprincipled pragmatism, doing whatever gets the desired results. It is essentially an attitude of anarchy, but it is very subtle. It can come across as an admirable and scrupulous knowledge of fine points of law. But it is always entirely selfish, providing a way for sinners to do whatever they want. It leans on some legal detail to justify an illegal activity. It was true 3,000 years ago, and it remains true now. Legalism to the rescue!

Legalism in the church

Of course legalism exists outside the church too. For

WHAT THE TEXT TEACHES

example, in the city of Bundaberg, a man was fined for driving a car in excess of the speed limit. He fought it in court. He never denied his excess speed. He accepted the accuracy of the police radar evidence against him. At no point did he deny breaking the law, but he was a legalist. He used the law to avoid the law. He argued the semantic technical detail that State Police radar operators were using transmitting devices under Federal Government Laws, requiring them to hold a Federal Government licence. But State Police hold a state licence. On that basis the State Police, though properly trained to operate the devices, were technically unqualified to operate the radar. He won his case. The law was used to avoid the law, and the central weighty matter of excessive speed was ignored. Legalism to the rescue! This is a classic example of straining out gnats and swallowing camels! But as common as legalism is in society, it is worse when it appears inside the church. It is then a sin against greater light, an aggravated iniquity.

The sad fact is that legalism is not uncommon in the courts and committees of the church. There are men whose supreme standard seems to be the 'Church Code' (constitution and procedures) rather than the Bible. Meetings can become virtual contests of legal chess, with much manoeuvring and counter-manoeuvring. Instead of biblical remedies being applied to problems, every possible legal 'spanner' is thrown into the works. Success comes not to him who is most biblically and theologically correct but to him who is most legally shrewd, legally opportunistic and legally semantic. The following unforgettable example concerns legalism and the 'call of nature'.

Debate was underway in the highest court of a certain church. There was a rule preventing anyone from voting on an issue if they had not heard all the speeches in the debate. It was a reasonable law designed to stop people voting in ignorance. Just as the last speaker was closing the debate, one delegate retired to the toilet. He returned a few minutes later just in time for the vote. At once a legal point of order was raised: 'This man cannot vote because he did not hear all the speakers as the law requires.'

What followed was legalism at its peak. For quite some time there was a debate about whether he could vote. The resident legalists thumbed through their codes and indexes to see if the law provided any relief for calls of nature. The final speaker said he was happy for the man to vote even though it was his speech that had been missed. But the legalists insisted on the letter of the law: 'It says in our law that if he does not hear the entire debate he cannot vote. He did not hear the entire debate and therefore he cannot vote. The law is clear. The words are clear. We insist that he cannot vote!'

By the mercy of God the man was allowed to vote, and the court ruled that going to the toilet was not illegal and did not limit his voting rights. Then the treasurer advised the assembly of the large sum of money that the foolish and legalistic debate had cost the church.

Jesus gave the answer to legalism when he suffered its attack:

> One of them, an expert in the law, tested him with this question: 'Teacher, which is the greatest commandment in the Law?' Jesus replied: '"Love the Lord your God with all your heart and with all your soul and with all your mind." This is the first and greatest commandment. And the second is like it: "Love your neighbour as yourself." All the Law and the Prophets hang on these two commandments' (Matt. 22:35).

Legalism has lost sight of the fundamental purpose for laws.

REMEMBER THIS

Laws are used to facilitate godliness and neighbourliness. The acid test for any rule, law, procedure or rationale is whether it is both godly and neighbourly? Is it consistent with my duty to love God supremely, and is it consistent with my duty to love my neighbour as myself? If so by all means follow it. If not then adopt a more suitable course. Laws are our servants not our masters. They are designed to expedite business in the church in a godly way. To the extent that they do so they are useful. To the extent that they preclude this they are useless and should be abandoned!

May God deliver us entirely from legalism! We are committed to *legality* but that is not the same as *legalism*. Let us aim at the weighty matters of love towards God and our fellow man. This is what all good law amounts to. Otherwise, if we are pedantic and legalistic it is a sign that we are not submitting to the rule of King Jesus. We are doing what is right in our own eyes just as in the days of the judges. Legalists advertise the spiritual barrenness of their own souls.

In closing

The appropriate attitude as we close the book of Judges is one of praise and adoration for the God of all grace. We have been privileged to think through an intriguing part of the Old Testament. Over and over again rebellious people committing atrocious sins have shocked us, yet they repeatedly received the amazing grace of God. The incredible patience and compassion of God stands out against the awful depravity of the human race. His mercy is beyond measure. It is just as true today. If God should mark iniquity none of us could stand. God is abundant in mercy, and when he gives it, it is never deserved.

We have seen how Christ is revealed in this book; not only by the appearances of 'the angel of the LORD' but also in the role that he plays in the progress of salvation history. The people needed a king. Anarchy had to give way to monarchy. Israel's judges gave way to Israel's kings. Israel's kings climaxed in Christ, the King of kings. This is the ultimate expression of God's mercy and grace. This is the King who came to serve his people. In the cross of Christ, God incarnate stood in for the guilty and suffered their curse. Commitment to him is the way to our eternal blessing. Anything less is trifling with all that is dear to God. This is very evident in the book of Judges. This is the gospel.

QUESTIONS FOR DISCUSSION

1. *'Legalism is a form of antinomianism.' Evaluate this statement in the light of Matthew 5:33–37.*

2. *What does God require regarding oaths and vows? Are they forbidden? (See Lev. 19:12; Deut. 6:13; 10:20; Ps. 15:4; 76:11; Matt. 5:33–37; Heb. 6:13–20.)*

3. *What is the real meaning and value of integrity? (See 1 Kings 9:4–7; 1 Chr. 29:17–19; Job 2:3; Ps. 7:8–10; 19:14; 24:3–6; 25:21; 41:12; 51:10,17; 78:72; Isa. 59:2–9; Matt. 22:16; Titus 2:7.)*

THE GUIDE

APPENDIX

THE MONARCHY: AN ISSUE RESOLVED

Question

How do we resolve the apparent difference between Judges and 1 Samuel 8? In Judges there was no king in Israel (so everyone did what he wanted), but when the people asked for a king in 1 Samuel 8, God was displeased.

Answer

The aged Samuel appointed his two sons, Joel and Abijah, as his successors to lead Israel. But they were corrupt (1 Sam. 8:1–3). So the elders complained to Samuel and demanded a king (8:4–5). There was something about this request that displeased both Samuel and God. It was not the request for a king *per se* that was problematic. Rather it was the motives and terms of that request. It was the *type* of king they wanted and the purpose for which they wanted him. Several features in the text show this.

First, they wanted a king in order to emulate the pagan nations: 'now appoint a king to lead us, such as all the other nations have' (8:5). They wanted political and military clout.

Second, the sort of kingdom that God intended for them was theocratic, where a godly man (like Samuel) ruled over Israel as God's anointed one. That was how God himself interpreted the situation for Samuel. Israel's model was a rejection of theocratic rule, a rejection of God as king: 'And the LORD told him: "Listen to all that the people are saying to you; it is not you they have rejected, but they have rejected me as their king. As they have done from the day I brought them up out of Egypt until this day, forsaking me and serving other gods, so they are doing to you"' (8:7-8).

Third, God spelled out in detail the terrible consequences of their request for a worldly king (8:9-18). Basically, the king would make himself rich and famous at Israel's expense. God assured them it would be a curse to them and that they would rue the day: 'He will take a tenth of your flocks, and you yourselves will become his slaves. When that day comes, you will cry out for relief from the king you have chosen, and the LORD will not answer you in that day' (8:17-18).

Israel's perverse response was predictable: 'But the people refused to listen to Samuel. "No!" they said. "We want a king over us. Then we will be like all the other nations, with a king to lead us and to go out before us and fight our battles"' (8:19-20). The last sentence confirms the interpretation above.

As the next chapter tells us, they got the type of king that they wanted: 'He had a son named Saul, an impressive young man without equal among the Israelites — a head taller than any of the others' (9:2). Saul was ungodly and a disaster for Israel. The true model of theocratic rule was exemplified in David and Solomon (though imperfectly) and ultimately in Christ, the perfect King.

THE GUIDE

NOTES

NOTES

Chapter 1: Understanding Judges (An overview)

1. It is also clear that the book was written after the Ark of the Covenant was removed from Shiloh (see Judg. 18:31; 20:27; 1 Sam. 4:3–11). The writer is describing events before the division into the Northern and Southern Kingdoms of Israel and Judah (ca 930 B.C.).
2. The words 'until the time of the captivity of the land' (18:30) are sometimes taken as a reference to the Assyrian captivity of Israel in 722 B.C. This would imply a much later composition of Judges. Two other possibilities should be noted. Even if it is a reference to the fall of Samaria a later editor could have inserted it in the original book. More likely, the 'time of captivity' refers to the Philistine domination of the land during the time of the judges. The Philistine problem is a major issue in the book, and Psalm 78:61 uses 'captivity' to describe it.
3. Four more examples of judge-deliverers are found in 1 Samuel: Eli, Samuel, Joel and Abijah.
4. Moses created the office of judge to help him govern the vast multitudes of Israel in the wilderness wanderings (see Exod. 18:21ff and Deut. 1:9ff). There the idea of 'magistrate' was prominent. Those judges were especially involved in settling legal disputes, as the Law of God was applied to daily issues.

Chapter 3: The angel of the LORD

1. More proof is also found in Judges 13 (with Samson's parents), Genesis 22 (with Abraham on Mt Moriah) and Genesis 32 (interpreted by Hosea 12), where Jacob wrestled with the man who is God.

Chapter 4: Christ: The angel of the LORD

1. Isaiah had already called him 'Immanuel' (עִמָּנוּאֵל), meaning *God with us* (Isa. 7:14).
2. John's words in John 1:21 do not contradict this. He denied that he was literally Elijah reincarnated.

Chapter 5: An old soldier and an oxgoad

1. See Numbers 13:28–33 and Deuteronomy 1:2; 2:10; 9:2. 'Anakim' means long-necked.
2. This is the aptly named title of Gary Inrig's commentary on Judges (Moody Press, 1979).

Chapter 6: A pointed message from God

1. See Deuteronomy 34:3.
2. They obviously had not met sporting champions like Rod Laver! He is the only tennis player in the world to win two 'Grand Slams'. He did it in 1962 as an amateur and again in 1969 as a professional. He was left handed.

Chapter 7: Barak and Deborah in concert

1. As early as the end of the second century Tertullian refers to Christian widows and the various ministries they performed. Some undertook a ministry of prayer support. Others nursed the sick, cared for orphans, visited Christians in prison, evangelized pagan women and catechized female converts in preparation for their baptism. (See the entry for 'Widows' in the *Encyclopaedia of Early Christianity* (E. Fergusson, Ed., St James Press, 1990) and the entry 'Assistance and Charity' in the *Encyclopaedia of the Early Church* (A. D. Berardino, Ed., James Clarke, 1992).
2. It is true that God had permitted them to settle east of the Jordan, but that did not mitigate their responsibilities towards the rest of Israel (see Josh. 1:12–15).

Chapter 11: Has Jephthah been defamed?

1. For a competent essay on this issue see Donald Macleod's 'Can God Suffer' in *Behold Your God*, Christian Focus Publications, revised edition 1995, pp.31–37.
2. This is exactly how the word is used in Deuteronomy 32:47, where Moses recites the Word of God to Israel and warns them not to treat it lightly: 'They are not just idle words for you — they are your life.' It is not unimportant or of minor status or consequence.
3. See 1 Samuel 22:1–2.
4. A 1973 edition of the NASV has 'or' with a note saying that 'and' is also possible.

Chapter 12: What about Samson? (Part 1)

1. See Exodus 34:11–16 and Deuteronomy 7:1–4.

Chapter 13: What about Samson? (Part 2)

1. Though animals are described as 'living souls' (נֶפֶשׁ חַיָּה) in Genesis 1:20,24 and in Leviticus 11:10, there is no ambiguity. In those places it is the animating principle that is in view. There *nephesh* is used in its most basic sense, referring to the breath of life that distinguishes the animate creation from the inanimate (vegetation). Otherwise the term 'soul' is used consistently and frequently (over 700 times) to designate human beings made in the image of God.

Chapter 14: Final flashbacks

1. Note the sarcasm of Isaiah in Isaiah 44:9–20 over this precise folly. As ex-priest Charles Chiniquy wrote when he came to realize the folly of transubstantiation in the Mass: 'Any god that can be eaten by the rats is no god' (C. Chiniquy, *Fifty years in the 'Church' of Rome*, Chick Publications, 1985, pp. 151–154).
2. For an explanation of why God was displeased when Israel asked for a king (1 Samuel 8) see the 'Appendix' on page 247.

Chapter 15: No king — do anything!

1. Shakespeare's *The Merchant of Venice* summed it up well: 'In religion, what damned error but some sober brow will bless it, and approve it with a text, hiding the grossness with a fair ornament.'
2. The downgrade is evident even in Reformed and Presbyterian churches that have been traditionally known for doctrinal purity. For example, from 9 to 16 June 2002, the 213th General Assembly of the Presbyterian Church USA (PCUSA) was held in Louisville, Kentucky, where the question of homosexual ordination was debated. Under scrutiny was section G-6.0106b from the book of church order, also known as the 'fidelity and chastity provision'. It states:

> Those who are called to office in the church are to lead a life in obedience to Scripture and in conformity to the historic confessional standards of the church. Among these standards is the requirement to live either in fidelity within the covenant of marriage between a man and a woman, or chastity in singleness. Persons refusing to repent of any self-acknowledged practice which the confessions call sin shall not be ordained and/or installed as deacons, elders, or ministers of the Word and Sacrament.

Regrettably, by a vote of 317 to 208, the General Assembly decided to repeal the 'fidelity and chastity provision'. Individual churches in the PCUSA were given one year to reject or affirm this vote by a majority decision. It is lamentable that 317 of the PCUSA's spiritual leaders have set themselves against the clear, condemnatory teachings of the Scriptures on homosexuality (whether in pulpit or pew) in order to further nebulous, wrongly defined and often contradictory appeals like 'unity in diversity'. It is also common knowledge that the Netherlands has Protestant Reformed churches with an official policy of welcoming practicing homosexuals to the Lord's Table.
3. For useful sources, see the informative article 'How We Went Gay' by Tony Payne in *The Briefing*, Issue 221/2, July 2, 1998, pp.6–12.
4. Abomination is designated by תועבה in the Old Testament and βδέλυγμα in the New.

Chapter 16: A stitch in time

1. The precise number of Benjamites is not clear. According to verse 15 there were 26,700 in the army. However, verse 35 records 25,100 casualties, whereas verses 44 to 47 indicate 25,600 (25,000 casualties and 600 survivors). Two likely factors explain the discrepancy. First, there were probably unrecorded numbers lost in the first two battles. Benjamin must surely have lost some men. But that number is not recorded. Second, they are probably 'rounded' numbers, not statistically precise demographics. We still quote war statistics or the population of a town or city in the same way.
2. Eric Turnbull, ISBN 0-949599-00-X, undated, printed by Franklin Printing and Litho Company, Sunshine Victoria.

Chapter 17: Legalism to the rescue!

1. Admittedly, this is not what most people would associate with the term 'legalism'. It is a term with many nuances. Literally it is 'strict adherence to law or formulated rules' (*Macquarie Dictionary*). Depending on the context, legalism can be positive (insisting on the rule of law rather than arbitrariness) or negative (a pedantic literalism that ignores the intent and spirit of the law). Even the former sense has its own negative nuance, depicting a litigious spirit that insists on its 'pound of flesh' or demands explicit 'chapter and verse' references for either warranting or prohibiting any action.

   In the field of theology the nuances multiply. A legalist believes a man can merit God's favour by obedience to the law. Pelagianism and Pharisaism are classic illustrations. However, the term 'legalist' is also used pejoratively against anyone who properly upholds biblical precepts. As Gordon Clark has written: 'In the present century the term legalism has been given a new meaning. Situation ethics (q.v.) despises rules and laws. Anyone who conscientiously obeys God's commandments is regarded as legalistic. Therefore Joseph Fletcher approves the breaking of every one of the Ten Commandments. He then transfers the evil connotation of legalism to the historical morality of Protestantism' (C. F. Henry, Editor, *Baker's Dictionary of Christian Ethics*, Baker Books, 1973, p.385).

   My approach in this book is more philosophical because I am attempting to expose the core issue behind every unbiblical nuance of legalism. My thesis is that legalism is essentially the using (or misusing) of law in order to avoid the proper actions enshrined in the law.